Glowing Through *What We* Go Through

A Memoir of Finding Light in Life's Adversities

Tejumade Ogunmokun

ISBN: 979-8-9925610-1-2 (Paperback)

ISBN: 979-8-9925610-0-5 (Hardcover)

ISBN: 979-8-9925610-2-9 (eBook)

Book design by Dara Publishing LLC

Place of Publication: Richmond, Virginia, 23224

Library of Congress Control Number: 2025902500

Printed in the United States of America.

Disclaimer: The publisher and the authors do not make any guarantee or other promise as to any results that may be obtained from using the content of this book. This publication is meant as a source of valuable information for the reader. However, it is not a substitute for direct expert assistance. If such a level of assistance is required, the services of a competent professional should be sought..

Dedication

To all the women in this world who have ever found themselves drained by helping others excessively—this book is for you.

I once found myself in your shoes, giving jump-starts to someone's car every single day until my own check engine light came on. It wasn't until I put my foot down and refused to continue enabling that behavior that the other person finally took responsibility and got their battery replaced.

In that moment, I learned a valuable lesson—you have to protect your own battery, your own energy, before you can effectively help others. Too often, we allow ourselves to be depleted while trying to lift up those around us.

No more. This book is a reminder that it's okay, and in fact necessary, to say no to those relationships or situations sometimes. To preserve your own power so that you can be fully charged and ready to show up as your best self. Your battery, your energy, is precious. Don't let anyone drain it at your own expense.

This story, and the wisdom it contains, is dedicated to you. May it empower you to set boundaries, to prioritize self-care, and to never again sacrifice your own well-being in service of others. Your light deserves to shine brightly. This book will show you how.

Table of Contents

Glowing through what we go through

Foreward

Dear Valued Reader,

"Nothing is ever shattered beyond repair." – **Tejumade Ogunmokun**

My name is Shakira Shepperson and I am a teacher who holds a degree in elementary education. I plan to pursue my doctorates in this field. Educating has always been my philosophy and true passion.

I currently homeschool my three amazing grandchildren, who are learning and growing daily. Watching them prosper every day with the knowledge I've embedded in them ignites the fuel to my fire. My love for literature and art positions me to view stories like this as a gift, as it holds a valued message.

Glowing Through What We Go Through is a book built on the principles of **G**od's **L**ove **O**ver **W**orry. The author, Tejumade Ogunmokun, exemplifies many great, heartwarming stories through her creative writing skills. We met while she was working for Uber. I was her passenger and we discovered so many things in common through our conversation with each other. The ride was so impactful and encouraging that I invited her to join the writers club for authors. Since then, we have been good friends. Therefore, it is with immense gratitude that I introduce you to her spiritually charged literary contribution.

As an educator and fellow creative, when asked to write this foreword, I had no idea that I would face my very own GLOW-up season. To be exact, it was six days after being asked that the currents of my life would experience a tsunami of heartache. I lost my father. He was a man of God who had led many souls to Christ. So it should have been no surprise that the Most High would have my path cross with this lovely woman of God. She is God's grace personified. Within these pages are well-written testimonies that will inspire and motivate you to acknowledge God's presence in your own life.

After reading the whole of this testament to the goodness of God, this page-turner had ministered to my heart in ways unexpected. With in-depth details shared, she validated my feelings and affirmed that I was not alone in my life's struggles. Further, by sharing so openly, Tejumade Ogunmokun awakened my praise, which had lain dormant in the wake of my father's death. As a result of her soul-stirring words of wisdom, I have come out on the other side of grief with an invaluable relishing of the Most High's authority in my life. To that end, it is well with my soul. Amen.

As one of today's most inspirational authors, Ms. Tejumade's words paint vivid pictures of her life's experiences, both devastating and joyous. You will find instance after instance where you relate to her plight and celebrate challenges overcome. Now, allow me to tantalize your anticipation with summarizing points of each chapter: you will be walked through the process of adjusting to change, accepting the heritage and power held within your name, acknowledging that God's heritage of childbearing is a gift given in His perfect timing, appreciating the removal of toxicity in disguise from your life, ascension into one's rightful place, attesting to the GLOW, affirming oneself as a perfected vision in God's redemption, and avowing that it all was for your good.

"Hope isn't something we feel, it is something we choose." –
Tejumade Ogunmokun

When an author takes time to pour their heart into their work, the evidence of such is produced through the deep connection that develops between the reader and the piece itself. This is surely the experience I had and am sure you will too. I believe this because Tejumade is a person of indebted character, simply because "If the Son therefore shall make you free, ye shall be free indeed" (John 8:36, KJV). She is free because she placed her hope in the unchanging hands of the Lord and He looked beyond her faults and saw her need.

So, as you read the following pages, allow yourself to receive the move of God shown in her testimonies. Take time to interact with the text. There are writing prompts at the end of each chapter that will lead you to self-discovery and healing. Trust yourself and know that it did not happen to you but rather for you. It happened to pressurize your process into the diamond you are destined to become.

Thank you for your time and patronage. May you be blessed beyond measure by the faithful hand of our Father in Heaven. Amen. Now, enjoy *Glowing Through What We Go Through*.

Sincerely,

Shakira S.

Glowing through what we go through

Introduction

L ife has a way of testing us, doesn't it? It throws curveballs, heartbreaks, and challenges we never imagined we'd have to face. But through it all, I've come to realize something profound: the very trials that seem designed to break us often reveal the strength we didn't know we had.

Welcome to *Glowing Through What We Go Through: Rising Above Adversity.* This is my story, but it's also yours. It's a story of pain, perseverance, faith, and triumph. It's about finding the power within to rise above life's challenges, even when the odds seem stacked against you.

I'm not here to tell you that my journey has been easy—it hasn't. I've faced the heartbreak of infertility, endured the sting of a friend's betrayal, navigated career setbacks, wrestled with spiritual confusion, and struggled with addiction. Each chapter of this book takes you through one of these pivotal moments in my life, moments that forced me to dig deep, rely on my faith, and discover a resilience I never thought possible.

My Journey Through Adversity

There were days when the weight of multiple miscarriages felt unbearable. I questioned everything—my body, my faith, my worth. But I didn't give up, and by God's grace, I experienced the pure joy of becoming a mother. It's a joy I now know was worth every tear and every prayer.

I've also had to learn the hard way that not everyone in your life is meant to stay. When a close friend betrayed me, I was devastated. Letting go of that toxic relationship was one of the hardest things I've ever done, but it was also one of the most liberating. Through that experience, I learned to trust God's plan for my life and to embrace the people who truly uplift me.

Career setbacks can feel like the ultimate defeat, and I've been there too. When my book was unjustly taken down from a major platform, it felt like all my hard work was unraveling. But instead of giving up, I fought back—with prayer, perseverance, and a little legal help. That chapter of my life taught me the importance of reclaiming my power and standing firm in my worth.

As if that weren't enough, I've discovered that addiction comes in many forms—shopping, social media, alcohol, or even relationships. For me, it was calling psychics. It may seem unusual, but the root cause was the same: I was looking outside of myself, and outside of God, for what I thought I lacked. I was seeking clarity, reassurance, and answers in places where they could never be found. Breaking free from that cycle wasn't easy, but it was necessary. Through prayer and surrender, I realized that the peace and direction I was searching for were already within me, gifted by God and waiting to be uncovered.

Through it all, one thing has remained constant: my faith in God. There was a pivotal moment when I surrendered everything—my plans, my fears, my doubts—to Him. That surrender wasn't easy, but it was the turning point that gave me peace and strength to face whatever came next.

Why I'm Sharing My Story

I'm sharing these stories with you because I know I'm not alone in these struggles. Maybe you've faced similar storms—moments that tested your spirit and made you wonder if you'd ever find your way through. I want you to know that you're not alone.

More importantly, I want you to know that there's hope. No matter what you're going through, you have the power within you to rise above it. And when you invite God into your journey, that power is magnified.

An Inspirational Moment

One night, at my lowest point, I found myself asking, "Why me, God? Why am I facing all these battles?" I sat in the silence, waiting for an answer, and what came to me was this: *"It's not why—it's who. Who will you become through this? Who will you help because of what you've endured?"* That moment changed everything. I realized my struggles weren't punishments; they were preparation. They were shaping me into someone stronger, wiser, and capable of helping others.

How to Use This Book

This book is more than a collection of stories—it's an invitation to reflect, grow, and glow. As you read, I encourage you to think about your own journey. What challenges have you faced? How have you grown through them?

At the end of each chapter, you'll find reflective questions and journaling prompts to help you dig deeper. Take your time with them. Use them as a guide to connect with your own strength, faith, and purpose.

And don't do it alone. Share this journey with someone you trust—a friend, a family member, or a support group. Talk about what resonates with you and what you're learning. There's power in community, and healing often happens in connection with others.

A Personal Invitation

I wrote this book to remind you that you're stronger than you think, braver than you feel, and more capable than you realize. No matter what you're going through, you can rise above it.

So let's take this journey together. Let's reflect, heal, and grow. Let's transform our trials into testimonies. Let's glow through the very challenges that once threatened to overwhelm us.

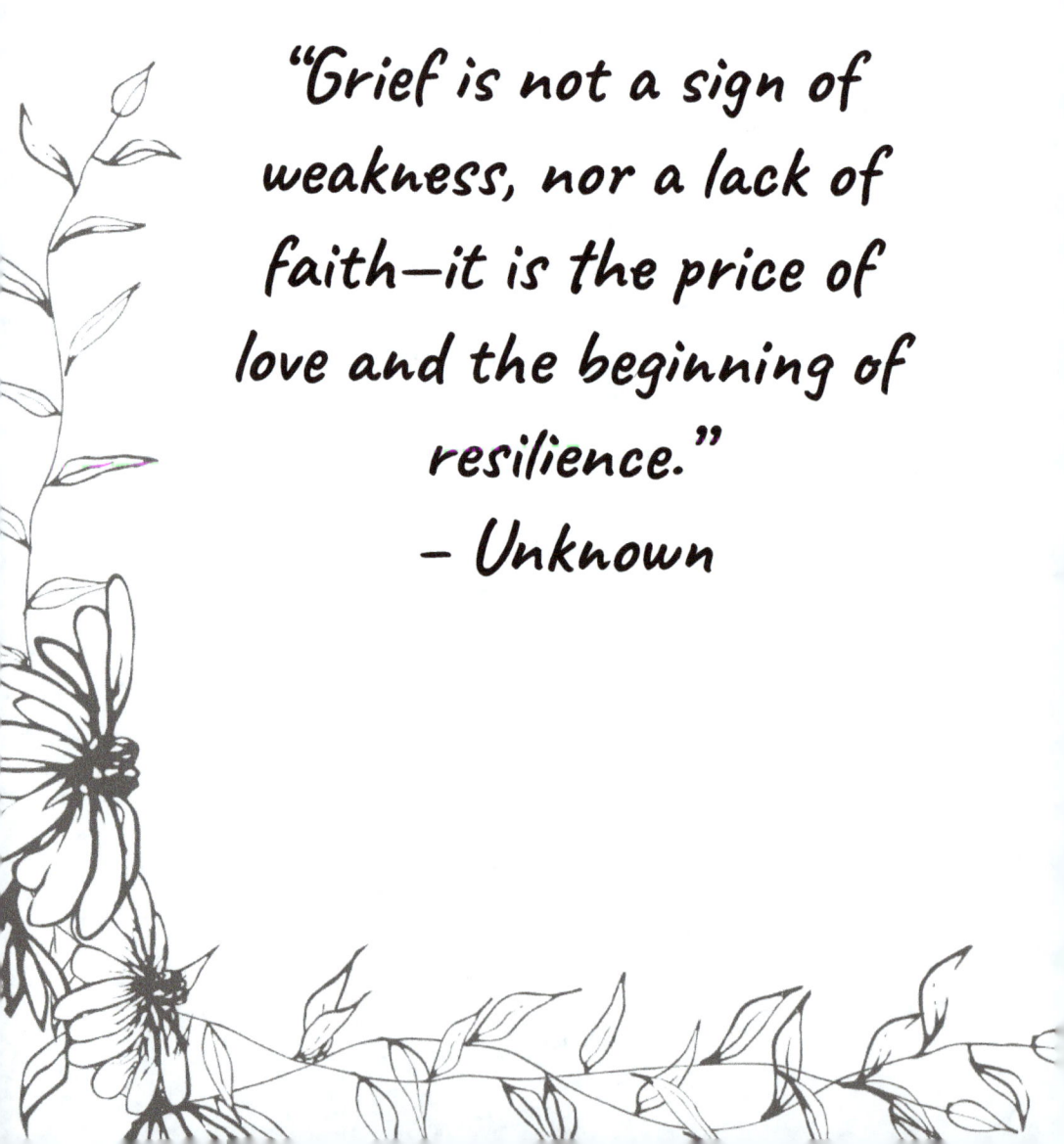

"Grief is not a sign of weakness, nor a lack of faith—it is the price of love and the beginning of resilience."
– Unknown

Chapter 1
Unfamiliar Territory
Grieving the Past, Embracing the Future

The move away from home was a bittersweet transition that would come to define a climactic chapter in my life. As a child growing up in the vibrant community of Long Island, New York, I had been blessed with a childhood filled with joy, laughter, and a deep sense of belonging. My sisters and I were well-known and loved figures in our neighborhood, our lives intertwined with those of our extended family and the tight-knit community that surrounded us. What I enjoyed the most about my upbringing was my grandmother Dorothy Lee; she was indeed the glue to our family. Going to her house every other day was a big part of my childhood. All of our cousins and family would be there, especially on Sundays. Grandma did not play—she lived directly behind the church and made sure all of her grandkids attended on Sundays, no excuses. I enjoyed being at church, sometimes singing in the kids choir, and last but not least getting candy from Sister Rose. Sister Rose was such a sweet old lady and she loved the kids. Anytime she saw us, she would immediately pull out her candy bag from her purse and pass it around to us. Seeing Sister Rose every week had us all on our best behavior because of course we loved candy. She had every candy you could think of. Peanut chews, Swedish fish, and my cousin's favorite: Mary Janes.

After church, Grandma would cook a nice Sunday dinner and we would all be gathered and merry. This was our bonding time. One of my favorite dishes was her macaroni and cheese. She showed me how to cut up the cheese and mix it into the noodles while adding milk and butter to it. She would look at me with so much happiness tickled with joy as she saw how eager I was to make the macaroni and cheese. It was always my absolute favorite day of the week growing up.

Another thing I loved about my upbringing in New York was how diverse our community was. Every culture and background was represented around us. From Hispanics, Italians, and Jewish people to Haitians, Filipinos, Caucasians, and African Americans, everyone was a part of the family and community and we all knew and had a natural love for one another. I didn't realize how big of an impact this diversity had in my life at the time. All I knew was that it was a part of who I was and I enjoyed it.

In that bustling, diverse environment, my unique name and cultural heritage were embraced as part of the rich tapestry that made up our community. Everyone seemed to know the Ogunmokun family, and we were welcomed with open arms wherever we went. My parents made sure to keep my sisters and I actively engaged in a variety of sports and extracurricular activities, further cementing our place within the fabric of our neighborhood. I remember spending long days outside, running around and having fun. You would find me playing double Dutch with my friends as we all took turns jumping in. My sisters each had their own thing, but everyone that knew me knew that double Dutch was all me! When you saw me jump in that rope, you would see me come to life. I did so many different tricks with my feet that everyone came to see my amazing footwork. I would bring the crowd and all the active girls in my neighborhood that loved sports would be alongside me. We were alive and in the moment. No judgment ever took place. We were just happy, active, carefree, vibrant kids of the neighborhood

18

that all got along with the one thing we had in common: the love for double dutch and many other sports. This was the time when SWV's "I Get So Weak in the Knees" and songs by Naughty by Nature, like "Feel Me Flow," were a hit. I remember it like it was yesterday—just the thought of this time makes me light up inside.

I was in my young prime years and I enjoyed every moment of it. My sisters and I would know it was time to come in when the street lights went off and our father came calling our names, sending us running for home.

Our dad's name is Taiwo, and back then, he had a very rich Nigerian accent because that's where he is from. So when he called us, we always were able to recognize his distinctive voice. He didn't play about his girls and often referred to us as his princesses. He would always tell us stories about how he is a king in Nigeria, should he go back one day and claim his throne. But until then, he would always make sure we knew that we were from a family of true royalty. He would dress us in nice garments of Kente cloth and other gorgeous, authentic, handmade fabrics from Nigeria, shipped directly from his mom and our grandmother, Chief Olori.

I used to love opening the boxes when they arrived in the mail. My sisters and I had plenty of beautiful garments and head wraps to match our dresses. We only wore them on Sundays when going to church. I remember one time we had an African fashion show. My dad was in charge of contributing some of his authentic pieces and garments to wear, distributing them amongst the models. It was absolutely beautiful! Everyone in our community was happy to be a part of this fashion show and loved all of the pieces shown. My mom and dad looked absolutely stunning in their blue dashiki clothes, which can be used as a wrap dress for women.

Looking back, those were truly carefree and pure times, a period of my life that I now recognize as a rare and precious gift. The warmth and acceptance I experienced during those formative years had shielded me from the challenges that lay ahead, lulling me into a false sense of security that would soon be shattered.

It was when my parents announced that we would be moving to Virginia that the first cracks in my idyllic world began to show. At the tender age of eleven, as I prepared to embark on the journey to sixth grade, I had no idea of the upheaval that awaited me. The familiar streets and friendly faces of Long Island would soon be replaced by an unfamiliar landscape, one that would test the very foundations of my identity.

I remember this day so vividly. It was a warm summer day as school was out. We were in the month of July, right around my birthday. We had come to the end of packing up all our belongings into the U-Haul truck. As we loaded the final item, we were met with our friends and family from the neighborhood known as "Homestead Village," greeting us with what felt like our final goodbyes to each other. The moment was bittersweet. Although I was excited for the journey of moving somewhere new, I was also very sad to leave a place I'd known since birth. After saying our goodbyes to our neighborhood family and friends, we then headed to one last stop.

When we arrived at my grandmother's house, this was when things got even harder. It was as if my world was slowly crumbling right before my eyes; at least that's how I felt.

I saw all of my cousins, aunts, and uncles, but the heaviest hit of them all was hugging my grandma. This was something we did daily and to know I was going to soon miss all of my grandmother's hugs and daily words of encouragement . . . it was a different type of feeling that I could not fathom. I was consumed with questioning my parents, wondering why we had to leave all of our family and friends behind. But although my thoughts and feelings were heard, I didn't think they mattered in this very moment because no matter how I felt, we were still headed to another state either way. At this moment, I went up to my grandmother and gave her a big old hug as she would always ask. She would always say—"*Come over here and give Grandma a big old hug and a big old kiss.*" And as I did so, she held me tight and said, "*Umm umm umm, that's my baby girl,*" as she hugged me. She told me she loved me and that she was only a phone call away. It was as if she could feel my hurt and pain, and as she said this to me, tears slowly ran down my face. I hugged her tighter as if I didn't want to let her go, but my father came in between us with a gentle tap on my shoulder, telling me it was time to go.

There I was, leaving my grandmother's house for the first time without knowing if or when I was coming back.

The ride to Virginia was monotonous and quiet. I was in deep thought as I looked out the window, admiring the scenery while on the highway. Once we passed the city part of New York, I felt like a part of me was being left behind as well.

Arriving in Virginia was like stepping into a completely different world. One day, I was surrounded by the bustling streets of New York, the hum of car horns, the chatter of neighbors in a dozen different languages, and the comforting aroma of my grandmother's Sunday cooking wafting through the air. The next, I was in Virginia—a place that felt too quiet, too still, and far too unfamiliar. It was as though someone had taken the vibrant, colorful tapestry of my life and replaced it with a blank canvas. I didn't know where to begin, and I wasn't sure I wanted to.

When we moved to a small town called Varina, I wanted to run far away. Coming from a busy, fast-paced environment to a slow, steady place with so much land and what looked like plantation fields was a drastic change for me. It was almost like we were in a movie. The environment was very southern and way too country for my liking. Everyone dressed and looked different, not to mention the mannerisms, completely unlike what I was used to. For instance, I never heard anyone say "pardon me" until I moved here. It also seemed like everyone had a persistent twang and their words were stretched out. And when I talked, everyone said I talked too fast and most people thought I was Hispanic when I spoke. Some people told me I sounded very proper. I don't know what they meant when they said I sounded proper, because all I was doing was speaking as I normally would. I guess they weren't used to my northern accent, the same as I wasn't used to their southern accent.

One thing for sure that I didn't like was what seemed to be a division. I noticed that in this town of Varina, it appeared the African Americans hung with African Americans and the Caucasians hung with the Caucasians. During this time, I was looking for all the Latinos, the Jewish, the Hispanics, the Indians, the Haitians, and the Filipinos but I didn't see them, or perhaps they were slim to none. The ethnically diverse backgrounds that I was used to were scarce, compared to the diversity I grew to love in my hometown of Long Island. I was sick seeing this. I just wanted to go back home—the home in my heart, not Virginia. In this moment, I felt lost and confused, like my parents were slowly stripping me of my identity simply by being here. I wanted my grandma, my cousins, and my northern friends back. I wasn't myself!

Back in New York, my world was full of life. Sundays were sacred in our family. My grandmother, the glue that held us all together, would host us every week. Her home was small, but it never felt that way. Cousins, aunts, uncles, and friends would cram into her living room, the sound of laughter and the clinking of plates filling the space. She'd make her famous sweet potato pie, and we'd sit around the table, sharing stories and teasing one another. My grandmother had this way of making everyone feel seen, like they belonged. She was the heart of our family, and when we left New York, I felt like I'd left my heart behind with her.

I missed my cousins, too. We were more like siblings than cousins, always getting into mischief together. I remember this one time, we decided to wander beyond the dead-end street that my grandmother always told us was the limit. On this particular day, we decided to take a long walk around the neighborhood while hanging out with our friends. Although our intent was innocent, we were only between the ages of nine and ten, so the fact that we disobeyed a known rule was pretty bad. However, we had a complete blast that day—we had so much fun that we even had the nerve to arrive back to my grandma's house late. Although it was late, we thought we had everything planned out! Our plan was to sneak into the house because it was late enough for her to be sound asleep. When we opened the living room door, we were so happy to see the lights were off because this confirmed she was indeed asleep. As soon as we stepped into the house, she surprised us by turning the lights on. Boy oh boy, Grandma had a rude awakening in store for us. As soon as that light switch went on, she set fire to our behinds. To make a long story short, we never went past that dead-end street again. Although we got into trouble, we couldn't help but burst out into laughter after the fact because we knew we were wrong and learned a valuable lesson that day.

Those were the kinds of memories that made New York feel like home—small, silly moments that meant everything.

Virginia, on the other hand, was a mystery. The streets were wide and empty, the houses spaced far apart. I remember standing in our new front yard, looking around and feeling like I was on another planet. Where were the bodegas? The corner stores? The people? It was so quiet that I could hear the wind rustling through the trees, something I'd never noticed in New York. At night, the silence was deafening. I'd lie in bed, staring at the ceiling, longing for the comforting noise of the city—the distant sound of a train, the murmur of voices outside my window.

School was another challenge. In New York, my classmates came from all over the world. We celebrated each other's cultures, and I never felt out of place. But in Virginia, I was one of the few kids who looked like me. I remember walking into my new classroom for the first time, clutching my backpack like a lifeline. The other kids stared at me, their eyes filled with curiosity and something else I couldn't quite place. I felt like an outsider, like I didn't belong.

One day, during recess, a group of girls approached me. "Where are you from?" one of them asked, her tone more accusatory than curious.

"New York," I replied. They exchanged glances, then burst into laughter.

"You talk funny," one of them said. I wanted to disappear. I wanted to run back to New York, to my grandmother's, to the life I knew.

Finding my identity in Virginia was hard. I felt like I was caught between two worlds: the vibrant, chaotic world of New York and the quiet, unfamiliar world of Virginia. I didn't know how to bridge the gap, how to make sense of who I was in this new place. I missed my family, my friends, and my culture. I missed the version of myself that existed in New York, the version that felt whole.

As I look back on the time after our move to Virginia, I now recognize the profound sense of grief that defined those days. At the time, I didn't have the words to name it—how could an eleven-year-old comprehend the weight of losing more than just a home? It wasn't just the streets, the friends, or the sense of community that I missed. It was the very essence of who I was in that familiar world. I didn't yet understand that leaving New York meant leaving a part of myself behind, one that I would spend years trying to find again in this new life.

Grief is often associated with losing someone we love, but in Virginia, I learned that grief can take many forms. I grieved the vibrant life I had known—the bustling energy of Long Island, the joy of Sundays at Grandma's, the simple comfort of belonging to a place where everyone knew me and my family. I grieved the version of myself that had existed there: confident, connected, and free. The quiet, sprawling streets of Varina, with their foreign rhythms, seemed to mock everything I had lost. I didn't know how to fit in, and worse, I feared that I never would.

The loneliness was palpable, but it also taught me how to sit with my feelings. It wasn't easy. At first, I resisted, burying my homesickness under layers of frustration and anger. I was angry at my parents for uprooting me, angry at my new school for being so different, and angry at myself for not being able to adapt more quickly. But over time, I began to realize that the only way forward was through. I had to acknowledge the sadness and allow myself to mourn what I had lost.

My journal became my lifeline. On its pages, I spilled my heart: memories of running through the streets with my sisters, the sound of Grandma's voice calling us in for dinner, the excitement of walking to the corner store with friends to buy candy. I wrote about how strange everything felt in Virginia—the accents, the slower pace, the stares that reminded me I didn't quite belong. Writing was a way to hold on to the pieces of my old life, to remind myself that those memories and experiences were still a part of me, even if they felt distant. I also wrote letters back and forth to my friends in New York. It brought so much joy to my soul to exchange letters with childhood friends and keep up with what they were doing back home. Writing became my way of holding onto the pieces of myself that I didn't want to lose. It was my way of finding my voice in a place where I often felt voiceless.

It wasn't just writing that helped me cope. Slowly, I began to open myself up to the new world around me. At first, it was small things: noticing the way the sunlight filtered through the tall trees in our backyard, listening to the hum of cicadas on warm summer nights, and marveling at the stars that seemed so much brighter here than in New York. These moments didn't erase the ache of missing home, but they gave me something to hold on to, a reminder that beauty could exist even in foreign places.

As I navigated this new terrain, I started to see that grief and adaptation often go hand in hand. To move forward, I had to let go—not of my memories or the love I carried for New York, but of the belief that my happiness was bound to one place. I had to accept that I could build something new without losing what I'd already had. This realization didn't come all at once. It was a slow, often painful process, filled with setbacks and moments of doubt. But each small step forward—whether it was making a new friend, finding a new favorite spot in town, or simply getting through a tough day—was a testament to my resilience.

Grandma's voice stayed with me throughout this journey. Her words, "I'm just a phone call away," became a mantra. Even from a distance, her presence was a source of comfort and strength. When I felt lost, I would remember her wisdom, her ability to find joy in simple things, and her unwavering belief in the power of family. I carried those lessons with me, and they became a guide as I learned to adapt to my new life.

Over time, I began to understand that the move to Virginia wasn't just about leaving something behind. It was also about discovering new parts of myself. I learned that I could survive—and even thrive—in the face of change. I discovered a resilience I didn't know I had, a strength that came from embracing the unfamiliar and finding ways to make it my own. I learned to see grief not as something to fear or avoid, but as a natural part of growth, a reminder of the love and connection that shaped me.

Now, when I think about that time in my life, I see it not just as a period of loss, but also as a period of transformation. It was a time when I learned what it means to adapt, to hold on to the past while making space for the future. It was a time when I discovered that home isn't just a place; it's a feeling, a collection of memories and relationships that we carry with us wherever we go.

To anyone facing a similar journey, I would say this: Give yourself permission to grieve. It's okay to miss what you've lost and to feel the weight of that loss. But don't let it hold you back. Open yourself up to the possibilities of what lies ahead. You are stronger than you think, and the lessons you learn in times of transition will stay with you forever. Grief and adaptation are two sides of the same coin, and through them, we find our way forward, carrying the best of our past into the future.

Reflective Pause
Finding Strength in Transition

Change and loss, though painful, have the power to reveal our inner strength and capacity for growth. As you reflect on the themes of grief and adaptability in this chapter, consider how your own experiences of change have shaped your journey. These questions are an invitation to honor your past, embrace the present, and nurture hope for the future.

❊ How do you navigate moments when you feel out of place or disconnected? What strategies have helped you adapt to new environments?

_____

_____

_____

_____

❊ What lessons or strengths have emerged for you during times of significant change or transition?

_____

_____

_____

_____

❊ Think about a time when you found beauty or joy in an unfamiliar place or situation. What allowed you to open yourself to that experience?

_____

_____

_____

_____

❊ How can you honor the parts of your past that you miss while still allowing yourself to grow and embrace what lies ahead?

_____

_____

_____

_____

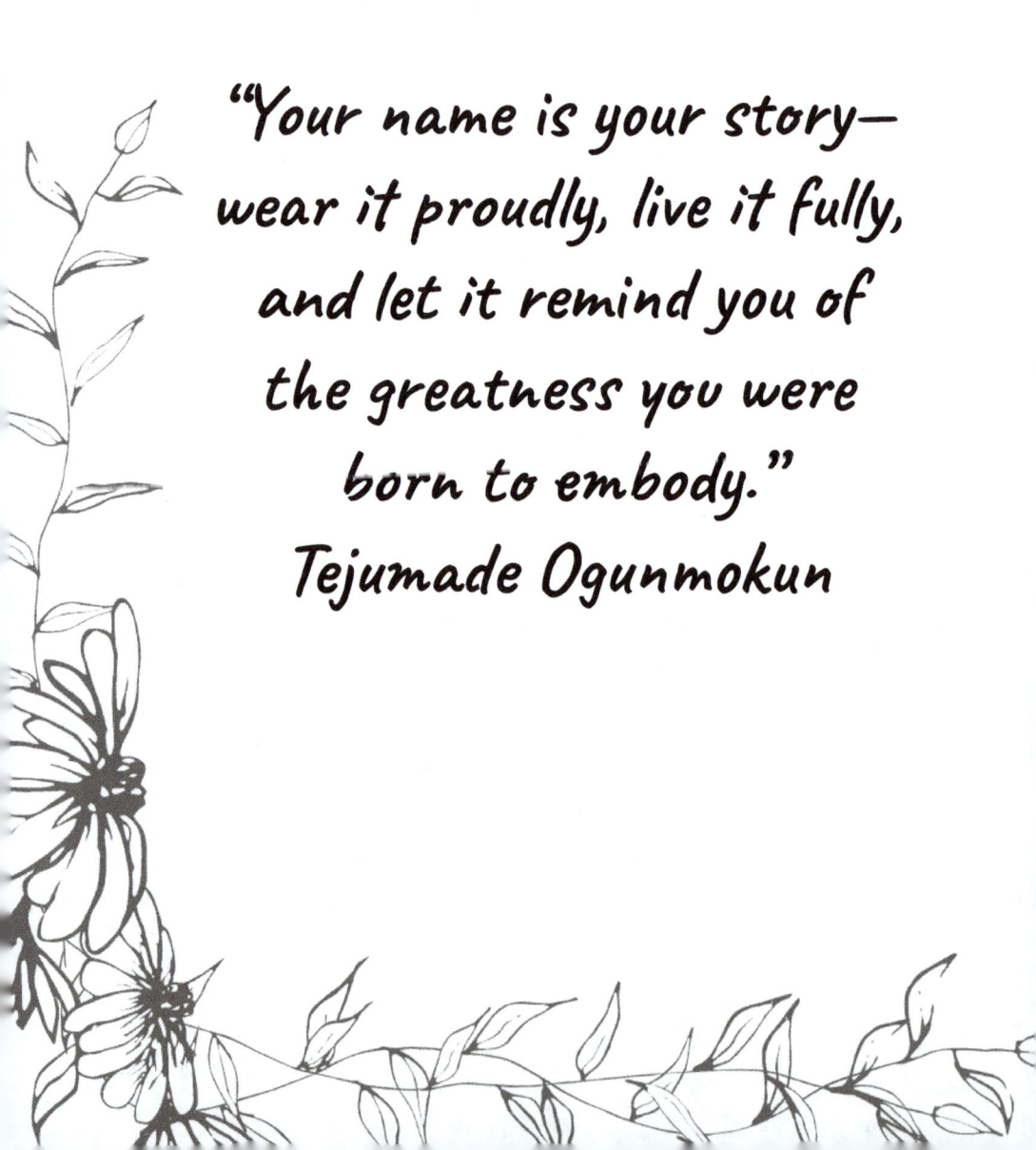

"Your name is your story—
wear it proudly, live it fully,
and let it remind you of
the greatness you were
born to embody."
Tejumade Ogunmokun

Chapter 2
The Power of a Name
Fix Your Gaze on the Crown

In Yoruba culture, a name is far more than an identifier; it is a proclamation of identity, a declaration of purpose, and a blueprint for destiny. The name Tejumade is a call to action, a directive to remain steadfast and focused on the ultimate goal—the crown. In Yoruba, "Teju" means "fix your gaze," and "ade" means "crown." Together, they form a name that is both poetic and powerful. It translates to "fix your gaze on the crown," a phrase that signifies focus, ambition, and the unyielding pursuit of greatness. To carry this name is to shoulder both the aspirations of my family and the legacy of a royal lineage.

But what does it truly mean to live up to such a name?

This chapter explores the profound meaning of names, the weight they carry, and how they shape our identity. It tells the story behind my name, Tejumade, and how I journeyed from resisting it to embracing it as a source of strength and guidance.

A Name with Purpose

My father, Taiwo, named me with intention. Coming from a royal family in Nigeria, he understood the weight and responsibility of a name. As the firstborn son of King Adelupa, he grew up immersed in the values of leadership, integrity, and service.

When it was time to name his child, my father saw an opportunity to pass down more than tradition; he wanted to instill a vision.

Naming me Tejumade was his way of reminding me daily to strive for excellence and embrace the values that defined our lineage. He believed that life is a journey, and the crown, whether literal or metaphorical, symbolized responsibility, wisdom, and a commitment to serving others.

Growing up, my father often spoke of my grandfather, King Adelupa, whose reign was marked by wisdom and progress. My father's stories weren't just family lore; they were lessons in leadership and purpose. I learned that my name wasn't just about me—it was about honoring the sacrifices and accomplishments of those who came before me. This understanding began to shape my identity, even as I wrestled with its implications.

The Struggle to Belong

As a child, the legacy of my name often felt more like a burden than a blessing. In a world that prizes conformity, my name set me apart in ways that felt isolating. It became a source of teasing and misunderstanding, and for a long time, I struggled to embrace it. I longed for the simplicity of names that blended in, not realizing that the very uniqueness I resisted was also my strength.

"Why is your name so long?" kids would ask, their curiosity often tinged with mockery. "Can't we just call you something else?" Their innocent questions stung, feeding my quiet longing to fit in, to erase the parts of me that marked me as different. I would fantasize about shortening my name to something simpler, more palatable—Teja or Mady—names that might let me slip into the crowd unnoticed.

Each time I voiced such desires, my father would meet them with gentle, unshakable resolve. "Your name is a gift, Tejumade," he would remind me. "It carries the strength of those who came before you. Changing it would diminish not just the name, but a part of who you are."

Reclaiming My Identity

It took years—and a journey of self-discovery—for me to reclaim my name. I had to dig deep to understand its meaning and the intention behind it. I had to reconcile the weight of my family's expectations with my desire to forge my own path. In doing so, I realized that my name was more than a reminder of my family's heritage; it was a reflection of my own purpose and potential.

A pivotal moment came during a school assembly when students were asked to introduce themselves and share the meaning behind their names. As my turn approached, anxiety threatened to choke me. I debated taking the easy way out—shortening my name, silencing the questions before they came.

But then, I looked into the crowd and saw my father's face. He wasn't speaking, but his eyes said everything: You are Tejumade. You are enough. You are more than enough.

I stood. My legs trembled, but my voice, steady and firm, carried the name my father had given me. "My name is Tejumade," I said, meeting every pair of eyes in the room. "It means 'fix your gaze on the crown.' It reminds me to carry myself with dignity, to embrace my strength, and to remember where I come from."

For a heartbeat, silence hung in the air. Then, applause. Among the crowd, I caught sight of my father. His face shone with pride, his thumb raised in silent affirmation. And as he stood to clap, like a domino effect, others stood across the auditorium to clap with him. In that moment, something shifted within me. My name, once a source of self-consciousness, became a badge of honor—a reminder of the strength, resilience, and love that shaped me.

Of course, life is a series of steps forward and back. The assembly was a moment of great progress for me, propelling me toward acceptance and pride in my name, but progress isn't linear and I had more challenges to face.

Junior high school was another battlefield for me. Not because of the classes or the homework, but because of my name—Tejumade. Every year on the first day of school, as the teacher called roll and I found myself yet again struggling to accept my name, I braced myself. I could see it coming, the hesitation, the furrowed brow, the awkward pause. "Tay-joo . . . Teh-joo . . . uh . . ." they'd stumble, and before they could butcher it further, I'd raise my hand and say, "It's Teh-ju-mah-day." But even then, the damage was done. The snickers from the back of the room, the whispered jokes, and the exaggerated mispronunciations would follow me for the rest of the day.

I remember one particular day in seventh grade when a boy named Ryan decided to turn my name into a game. "Hey, Teh-joo-made-a-mistake!" he shouted across the cafeteria, and his friends erupted in laughter. My cheeks burned as I tried to focus on my lunch, but the tears were already welling up. I wanted to disappear. I wanted to be anyone but Tejumade at that moment.

That night, I came home and threw my backpack on the floor. My dad noticed immediately that something was wrong. He always had this way of reading my emotions before I even said a word. "What happened, my princess?" he asked gently, sitting me down at the kitchen table.

Through tears, I told him about Ryan and the teasing. I told him how I hated my name, how I wished I could just be "Jessica" or "Emily" like the other girls. My dad listened patiently, his face calm but serious. When I was done, he reached across the table and took my hand.

"Tejumade," he said, his voice steady and full of warmth, "do you know what your name means?"

I nodded, sniffling. "Fix your gaze on the crown."

"That's right," he said. "Your name is a reminder of who you are and who you are meant to be. You are royalty, my princess. And royalty does not bow to the opinions of others. When they tease you, when they mispronounce your name, they are showing their ignorance, not your worth. You must fix your gaze on the crown and keep walking tall."

This steady encouragement from my father gave me the confidence I needed to move forward. His words stayed with me, and I allowed them to change my perspective and outlook on my name. I began to see it not as a burden, but as a gift. My name was a story, a legacy, a connection to my roots. It was a reminder of my strength and my purpose.

The next day at school, when Ryan started up again with his jokes, I stood up from my seat and looked him straight in the eye. "My name is Tejumade," I said firmly. "It means 'fix your gaze on the crown.' Maybe if you spent less time making fun of me and more time learning something, you'd understand how important names are."

The cafeteria went silent. Ryan looked stunned, and for the first time, I saw a flicker of embarrassment cross his face. He muttered something under his breath and turned back to his friends, but the teasing stopped after that. I had found my voice, and I wasn't going to let anyone take it from me again.

Eventually, I turned those tears into power. I took the time to enlighten others about who I was and where I came from. I shared the meaning of my name, the culture it represented, and the pride I carried in my heritage. Slowly but surely, I noticed a shift. People began to understand me better, and with understanding came respect. My name was no longer a source of ridicule—it became a conversation starter, a bridge between worlds.

Looking back now, I realize that those moments of teasing were not just challenges; they were opportunities. They taught me resilience. They taught me to stand up for myself. And most importantly, they taught me the power of a name.

Lesson Learned: Fully Embracing My Name

Fast forward to adulthood, I've come to realize the full weight and beauty of my name, Tejumade. It's no longer just a name— it's a story, a mission, and a reminder of the strength that flows through me. As I've grown into the woman I am today, my interactions with others have solidified the significance of my name in ways I never expected.

Meeting new people often begins with their fascination and curiosity about my name. "What does it mean?" they ask, leaning in with genuine interest. And every time, I take pride in explaining. This explanation is no longer a defensive act or a reluctant retelling—it's an opportunity to share the essence of who I am.

Over time, I've learned that my name has a way of sparking conversations, of creating connections. Some people are inspired by its meaning, using it as a reminder to pursue their own crowns—whatever they may be. Others are drawn to the culture it represents, eager to learn more about Yoruba traditions. Through these exchanges, I've become not just a bearer of the name but an ambassador for its message.

One particular encounter stands out in my memory. A colleague once asked me, "Does your name influence the way you see yourself?" The question struck me deeply. After a moment of reflection, I smiled and said, "Absolutely. My name is my compass. It reminds me to stay focused on what truly matters and to carry myself with the dignity of someone who is striving for greatness."

In that moment, I realized that my name had become an integral part of my identity—not just a legacy passed down from my father, but a purpose I had fully embraced. The teasing from my youth, the moments of self-doubt, and the struggles to belong—they were all necessary steps on my journey to understanding and living out the power of my name.

Fixing My Gaze on the Crown

Today, I walk with the confidence of someone who knows exactly who they are. I no longer flinch at the mispronunciations or the curious stares. Instead, I see them as opportunities to teach, to connect, and to inspire. My name, Tejumade, is no longer just a name—it's a testament to my strength, resilience, and unwavering focus.

If there's one message I want to leave with you, it's this: Embrace the fullness of who you are. Your name, your identity, your story—they are all uniquely yours, and they are all powerful. Whether your crown is a literal one, a dream you're pursuing, or a sense of purpose you're discovering, never lose sight of it. The journey won't always be easy. There will be moments of doubt, of misunderstanding, and of challenge. My father told me so many years ago the meaning of my name, and he told me to keep walking tall.

And so, I walk tall. With my name, with my heritage, with my purpose. I walk tall, knowing that every step I take is guided by the meaning and mission of the name I carry. I am Tejumade, and I have fixed my gaze on the crown.

Reflective Pause
Fixing Your Gaze on the Crown

In life's race, staying focused on your purpose and ultimate reward is essential. As you reflect on this chapter, take time to consider how you can align your actions, mindset, and faith with your higher calling. These questions will guide you in keeping your eyes fixed on the crown that awaits you.

✳ What does your name mean to you, and how does it reflect your identity or values?

_____

_____

_____

✳ Are there parts of your identity that you have struggled to embrace? How can you take steps towards owning them fully?

_____

_____

_____

✳ When was the last time you felt truly proud of who you are? What contributed to that feeling?

_____

_____

_____

✳ How do you define your "crown"? What goals, values, or aspirations keep you focused and motivated?

_____

_____

_____

✳ What story do you want your life to tell, and how does your unique identity contribute to that narrative?

_____

_____

_____

"Weeping may endure
for a night, but joy comes
in the morning."
– Psalm 30:5

CHAPTER 3
From Heartache to Hope

A Journey Through Infertility

The Silent Struggles We Carry

Gabrielle Union, the well-known actress, faced a deeply personal struggle with infertility and multiple miscarriages. For years, she and her husband, Dwyane Wade, tried to have children but were unsuccessful, and Union went through the emotional pain of multiple failed attempts. During her journey, she opened up about the profound grief of not being able to conceive, which was something she had dreamed of for most of her life.

Union has spoken openly about her journey, explaining how it tested not only her emotional limits but also her marriage and sense of self. She eventually turned to IVF (in vitro fertilization), and after several attempts, she and Dwyane Wade welcomed their daughter via surrogate in 2018. In her book *We're Going to Need More Wine*, Gabrielle speaks candidly about her struggles with infertility and the pain of not being able to have a child in the way she had envisioned.

What's powerful about Gabrielle Union's story is her transformation. She talks about the role of hope, faith, and the support of her family and community in helping her heal through the emotional toll of infertility. She found strength in her resilience and the love around her, ultimately giving her the hope to keep going and to accept a different, but fulfilling, form of motherhood.

Infertility is a deeply personal and often silent struggle, yet it's a reality faced by millions of women and families around the world. The emotional weight can be overwhelming, leaving many to wrestle with feelings of inadequacy, guilt, and despair.

For those who've walked this path, the experience is not just about the absence of a child—it's about the loss of dreams, the uncertainty of what lies ahead, and the unrelenting question of "why me?" Consider the countless women who've found themselves in this liminal space, longing for the joy of motherhood while enduring the heartbreak of loss. Their stories are varied, yet the pain is universally profound.

Take, for instance, the countless stories we hear of women who face the bittersweet cycle of hope and grief. From the moment they see a positive pregnancy test to the crushing loss that follows, the emotional journey is as unique as it is universal. Many describe feeling as though they're failing at something fundamental, as if their bodies are betraying them.

What is perhaps most remarkable, however, is the resilience these women show. Their stories teach us that even in the darkest moments, hope is a force that cannot be extinguished.

Connecting to My Journey

Like so many others, my journey through infertility brought me to the brink of despair. Each miscarriage felt like a chapter in a book I didn't want to write—a story of grief and uncertainty that I couldn't seem to close. There were moments when I questioned my body, my worth, and even my faith.

But through those moments, I discovered something I didn't know I had: an inner strength that refused to let me give up. Like the women who inspired me—those who found a way to carry on despite their heartbreak—I learned that hope isn't just something we feel; it's something we choose.

In the pages that follow, I'll take you through my journey—a deeply personal account of navigating the storm of infertility and finding light on the other side. But before we begin, I want to acknowledge the strength it takes to face these challenges, whether you're living through them yourself or walking alongside someone who is.

A Trip Down Memory Lane

As I reflect on my own journey, I'm reminded of the countless nights I spent grappling with the weight of unanswered prayers and unfulfilled dreams. The story of my battle with infertility is one of heartbreak, resilience, and faith. This journey tested my limits and redefined my understanding of hope. When going through the journey with infertility, it can often feel like walking through a relentless storm, where each wave of disappointment crashes harder than the last. Each miscarriage I experienced felt like a personal betrayal, an assault on my hopes and dreams, leaving me to grapple with a sea of unanswered questions and profound grief.

The First Miscarriage

The first miscarriage was the hardest. I remember the moment vividly—standing in the bathroom, staring at the positive pregnancy test, my heart racing with a mix of joy and trepidation. The excitement of seeing those two pink lines was overwhelming. I had envisioned a future filled with the laughter of a child, and in an instant, it seemed that future had been snatched away. When the bleeding began, it felt as though my world was collapsing.

The physical pain was excruciating, but it was the emotional turmoil that left the deepest scars.

Each day after that loss felt like wading through molasses, every step weighed down by an overwhelming sense of loss and emptiness. My relationships, once vibrant and full of life, began to feel strained. Friends who couldn't understand the depth of my grief inadvertently added to my isolation, leaving me feeling like an outsider in my own life. I watched as others celebrated their pregnancies, their joy a stark reminder of what I had lost.

I remember feeling so hurt every year during Mother's Day. The feeling was so painful that I found myself drained in sorrow, doubt, pity, and repeatedly questioning God. "Will I ever have a child?" I didn't know why or when it would be my turn to finally be a mother. All I knew was that I longed for a child and didn't feel complete. The feeling of something essential missing from my life was a constant ache. It was as if I was missing a crucial piece of myself that only motherhood could complete.

Self-Perception, Internal Conflict, and Doubts

As the miscarriages piled up, so did my internal struggles. My self-perception took a severe hit. I began to question my worth, wondering if my body was failing me in the most fundamental way. The repeated losses led to a deep-seated belief that perhaps I was not meant to be a mother, or worse, that I was being punished for something I couldn't even grasp. The mirror became an enemy, reflecting not just my physical changes but also the internal disarray that had taken hold. Each reflection reminded me of a dream that seemed increasingly out of reach.

The more I tried to mask my pain with a brave face, the more disconnected I felt from the person I used to be. It was as though each miscarriage had stripped away a layer of my identity, leaving me exposed and vulnerable.

The internal battle was relentless. Doubts gnawed at my sense of self, and my faith seemed to waver with each passing miscarriage. I found myself questioning whether I had the strength to endure another loss. The hope that once fueled me now felt like a distant memory, replaced by a growing sense of despair. I would often retreat to a quiet corner of my house, alone with my thoughts, and wonder if there was any light left at the end of this seemingly endless tunnel.

In these quiet moments, I was confronted with my deepest fears and insecurities. I questioned whether I was failing not just as a prospective mother but as a person capable of handling life's adversities. These moments of vulnerability were raw and revealing, laying bare my innermost fears and struggles. It was during these times that I grappled with my own worth and the impact of my losses on my sense of self.

Rebuilding Hope

Yet, in the darkest moments, I found unexpected sources of solace. Journaling became a lifeline, a way to pour out my pain and seek understanding. The act of writing allowed me to process my emotions and find some semblance of order in the chaos. Therapy provided a safe space to navigate the complex emotions of grief and gain perspective. My support system, though at times imperfect, offered a sanctuary where I could express my pain without judgment. The understanding from a close friend who had faced similar struggles became a source of comfort, reminding me that I was not alone in this fight.

Through the storm of trauma, I learned to rebuild my hope. Each miscarriage taught me something new about myself—about strength, resilience, and the capacity to endure. The emotional rollercoaster was relentless, but it also revealed a wellspring of inner strength I had not known existed. I discovered that resilience is not about never falling but about finding the strength to rise each time we do.

The path was long and arduous, but it led me to a place of profound personal insight and renewed faith in the possibility of a future filled with joy. I learned to find meaning in the suffering, using it as a catalyst for deepening my empathy and understanding.

As I moved forward, I realized that my journey through infertility, while marked by heartache, also illuminated the incredible capacity for hope and recovery. The path to healing is not straightforward, but it is possible. Each step, no matter how small, is a testament to the strength within us. By embracing our vulnerabilities and seeking support, we can transform our heartache into a source of inspiration and resilience.

In sharing my story, I hope to offer a beacon of hope to those who may be struggling with similar challenges. The road to healing is filled with obstacles, but it also offers moments of profound growth and renewal. My journey, though fraught with difficulties, has shown me that even in the midst of great pain, there is always a path to hope and a possibility for a brighter future.

Looking back on the year 2015, there I was, at the age of 32, looking at my two sisters and friends who had beautiful children they absolutely adored. I was the amazing auntie, daughter, sister, and friend who took my niece, nephew, and many other children under my wing, but I still felt a sense of voidness. The sensation of being on the outside looking in, despite being surrounded by so much love, was both painful and discouraging.

At that time, people would ask me, "Tejumade, when are you going to settle down and have some kids?" All I could think of was, the nerve of them to ask me such a personal question when they don't even know my story or pain. Little did they know that question cut me like a sharp knife to the heart. My response would be "when God blesses me" and I would kindly walk away. It was a beautiful vision to think about, but I couldn't help thinking of where I was at that very moment, longing and yearning to fill that present void that I felt.

I remember feeling nauseous, tired, and unable to stand the smell of many things, especially smoke. My cravings were intense and unpredictable. While grocery shopping, something prompted me to take a pregnancy test. My best friend, who I was talking to on the phone, encouraged me to pick one up. Initially, I reached for the cheapest test available, but she insisted I get the Clear Blue test because it was digital and reliable. Despite my hesitation about the $19 price, she promised to give me the money back, so I bought it.

Back home, I took the test while still on the phone with my best friend. When the test displayed the word "PREGNANT," my heart skipped a beat. I felt a rush of excitement mixed with disbelief and fear. Could this be real? After all the struggles and heartbreaks, was I finally pregnant? The significance of this moment hit me hard. I thought about my partner and what this news would mean for us. It was a glimmer of hope amidst the years of uncertainty and pain. I confirmed the result for my best friend, feeling the weight of this potential new chapter in our lives.

Eight weeks later, I had a scheduled ultrasound appointment at the "Pregnancy Resource Center." A friend had told me about this place, a perfect alternative because it was free, as my insurance hadn't kicked in yet. It was September 2015, and I was filled with joy and excitement to finally get a glimpse of my child. I had already tested positive for pregnancy and was approximately eight weeks pregnant. My boyfriend, who was just as excited, was by my side for support. This day was very special to us.

I vividly remember him holding my hand in the waiting room, the sense of excitement and nervousness palpable between us. "Ms. Tejumade," I heard the doctor call my name. "Yes," I said with excitement and nervousness as I stood up and walked back with her to our room. As we sat down, she looked at me while glancing at my medical chart. She went over basic questions prior to the ultrasound tech coming in, asking for permission to disclose certain things with my boyfriend present. I advised that it was fine, and she proceeded with caution.

She then paused and took a deep breath. "Tejumade, I see you've had several pregnancies but no births, is this correct?" I answered yes, looking at the doctor and then at my boyfriend, who held my hand tighter with urgency and compassion. My palms grew sweaty with anxiety. "So this would make your fourth pregnancy, is that correct, Tejumade?" I said yes. The questions were tedious, but I was confident that this was going to be a brighter day filled with greatness.

We were then guided to another room to wait for the ultrasound technician and the doctor. As I lay back in the chair, the technician approached me with a transducer device, explaining what she was about to do. She placed gel on it, advising me of the cool sensation as she prepared to insert the transducer into my cervix. The sterile smell of the ultrasound room, the cold gel on my abdomen, the sound of the technician's voice as she tried to stay calm—all these details are etched into my memory. She moved the object around my uterus, snapping pictures, mumbling to herself, "This can't be right." Concern filled the room as silence settled in. "Is everything okay?" I asked. "Yes, dear, I'm just trying to get a better view," she replied.

My boyfriend, across from me, looked at me with worry. The doctor asked him to step outside. The technician began a transabdominal ultrasound, moving the transducer around my abdomen. They gathered pictures from both ultrasounds and examined them together. I sensed something was wrong from their somber expressions.

The doctor and technician stepped outside, returning after ten minutes. "Hello, Tejumade, we're back. I'm afraid we have some news to tell you." My heart dropped, beating loudly in my chest. "We thoroughly examined the ultrasounds, and there appears to be no fetus found. I'm terribly sorry, Tejumade. We encourage you to consult with your OBGYN, Dr. Jones, as soon as possible for follow-up."

If you've ever felt the sting of an empty cradle, you know the pain that words can hardly capture. You're not alone in this journey. I burst into tears, running out of the office screaming, "NOOOO!" Shaking, my boyfriend met me at the elevator, holding me as I cried. I couldn't believe I was going through this again, with no answers or understanding. I felt utterly vulnerable, like a child lost in a vast, dark forest, unsure of which way to turn. The weight of my failures pressed down on me, and I wondered if I would ever find my way out. I was frightened, scared, humiliated, embarrassed, shocked, and most importantly, disappointed in myself. I felt like a complete failure.

Have you ever felt like your world was crumbling around you, leaving you powerless to stop it? Have you ever found yourself questioning everything you thought you knew about yourself? That's where I was, standing in that ultrasound room, my heart in pieces. Looking back, I realize that my sorrow wasn't just about losing a pregnancy; it was about losing a dream, a future I had painted so vividly in my mind.

The very next day, I was able to schedule an emergency appointment with my OBGYN, Dr. Jones. She was able to confirm with me that I had a spontaneous abortion. I wasn't quite sure what that was, but she thoroughly educated me on it while guiding me towards my next steps. Dr Jones was very knowledgeable and compassionate about her job. Every time I met with her, she had the ability to show me that she cared by going above and beyond to provide knowledge and education while guiding me through my troubling situation.

Have you ever met someone for the first time and instantly felt connected to them?

She had a mothering glow to her. I genuinely trusted her opinion and listened to her insight. She talked me into having a laparoscopic surgery to see why I kept having these miscarriages around the same time frame (seven to eight weeks.) Although I was scared, she advised me of the importance of this surgery if I wanted to know what's going on with my body. Once she broke things down for me, I agreed to proceed with the laparoscopy. Before concluding my visit, she left me with some pamphlets of information concerning the surgery which gave me a clear understanding. She scheduled me for a date two weeks out, which was enough time to prepare my job and family.

After my visit with Dr. Jones, I felt a slow restoration of hope. I began to regain my confidence, knowing that I was on the right track. Later that day, I excitedly shared everything with my boyfriend, sisters, and family. Informing everyone about the upcoming surgical procedure was a huge relief. Their support made me feel even better. Having that support and guidance from loved ones was very therapeutic and uplifting.

Two weeks passed, and today was the day of my surgery. My dad, older sister, and aunt drove with me. We met Dr. Jones in the waiting area. "Hey, Ms. Lady, are you ready?" Dr. Jones asked cheerfully.

"I am as ready as I can be," I replied. I gave my family warm hugs before walking with Dr. Jones to the prep room. I was briefed on the procedure and instructed to change into a hospital gown. After changing, I was met by five other doctors and surgeons. Dr. Jones stayed by my side the entire time. The last thing I remember her saying was that I would feel sleepy due to the anesthesia.

After the surgery, I woke up to everyone excitedly exclaiming, "She's up! She's up!" I was confused as to why everyone was so excited that I had woken up. Dr. Jones explained that it took a bit longer for the anesthesia to wear off, which was perfectly normal.

As I looked up from the surgery bed, I asked if we were done while facing my doctor. To my surprise, the surgery was complete. I was shocked because I couldn't remember anything other than being told I would become tired.

Dr. Jones confirmed, "Everything went well!" The fibroids blocking my tubes were removed, and the surgery was a complete success! She later advised me with urgency to contact her as soon as I became pregnant in the future. With the fibroids removed, I was informed that I had a much higher chance of maintaining my pregnancy past eight weeks. The miscarriages were due to the size and location of the fibroids, which were blocking my fallopian tubes and uterine cavity. Hearing all of this great news was truly inspiring.

Doctor Jones followed up with prompt instructions to rest for four weeks while avoiding lifting or bending. I was fascinated at the fact that I could not do certain things. "Are you serious? You mean I can't do my squats?" I asked hysterically, still under the effects of the anesthesia. I remember feeling woozy, as if I were floating on clouds.

My sister chuckled at my concern, while further reminding me I had bigger things to worry about. Although I agreed, the anesthesia had me feeling woozy and probably saying things that I normally would not have. Dr. Jones cheerfully advised my sister and family that the anesthesia would take some time to wear off and to monitor me closely.

Although I was sore and a bit out of it from the anesthesia, knowing the surgery had been successful was incredibly reassuring. Despite the numerous miscarriages and losses I had endured, this day filled me with hope and encouragement for the future. My family later brought me beautiful flowers and a cute, cuddly teddy bear. My road to hope and recovery had begun.

The biggest surprise was who truly supported me throughout this process. From the planning stages to the actual surgery, I found myself evaluating who was genuinely there for me.

As I recovered and got back to my normal self post-surgery, I realized that the person I expected to be there was nowhere to be found. My boyfriend was absent, which hurt deeply. It was my family and closest friends who showed up. Reflecting on these details, alongside what God had revealed to me, I understood that it was time to move on. Despite the difficulty of letting go, I felt that God was showing me there was more in store for me. To receive my blessings, I needed to let go, so I listened to God and did not fight the process.

Fast forward to a few years later, October of 2017 to be exact. During this time, I was a completely healed and restored woman. I took the necessary time to focus on myself, which consisted of living my best life and truly loving myself. While in this new era of my life, I met someone who captured my heart.

We met through a mutual friend at a photoshoot. As I was modeling, he was capturing photos of me. There was an undeniable connection when we locked eyes. After the shoot, I asked him to send me the pictures and videos, and when I saw them, I was impressed. Weeks later, we went on a date and have been inseparable ever since.

Have you ever felt like you already knew someone you met for the very first time? The connection between us was so deep, it felt as though I had known him all my life. We did everything together, shared countless laughs, prayed for each other, and enjoyed each other's company. It was like a breath of fresh air. Family and friends noticed the new glow in me and often asked what made me smile so brightly. Our bond was evident to everyone. The love felt true, genuine, and real, and I wanted more of what he gave.

Two years into our loving, growing relationship, I missed a cycle in early March 2019. I couldn't help but think about how passionate Valentine's Day had been. I wondered if this could be happening again. Although I knew what a missed cycle could mean, I tried not to get my hopes up due to past experiences. I was cautious but scheduled an appointment with Dr. Jones, remembering her advice to contact her immediately if I thought I was pregnant again.

When I called, I learned that Dr. Jones had moved to Florida, and I was referred to a new doctor in the same practice. Although I was saddened by this news, I proceeded with the appointment with the new doctor, who was highly recommended and familiar with my medical history. I greeted him with a mere hello, feeling that no one could understand my journey like Dr. Jones had.

He introduced himself and gestured to shake my hand. I wasn't impressed, as my mind was still set on Dr. Jones. However, the new doctor's positive demeanor and professionalism gave me a glimmer of hope.

The new doctor asked me to take a urine test, which showed positive results. He asked about my last menstrual cycle and estimated that I was about eight to nine weeks pregnant. He recommended a blood test and a cervix check for accuracy. As he left the room, I called my partner to share the news. Hearing his excitement filled me with joy, and he promised not to share the news until I was ready.

Three months later, we surprised our family and friends with the gender reveal. I had hoped for a girl, but the ultrasound revealed a healthy baby boy. While initially disappointed, I was overjoyed to have made it this far in my pregnancy. Seeing the excitement on my partner's face was deeply gratifying. I felt complete and excited about our future together.

We shared our ultrasound pictures, and the outpouring of love and congratulations from family and friends was overwhelming. I felt God's presence and realized His timing was perfect.

Throughout my pregnancy, I laughed and enjoyed every moment. My partner kept me laughing, even when I wanted to cry. I discovered his humor and found comfort in his presence. Sharing my pregnancy journey with a good friend who was also expecting made the experience even more special. We bonded over every aspect of pregnancy, from stretch marks to cravings.

Despite the joy, I experienced moments of doubt. I requested additional appointments and ultrasounds to ensure everything was okay. My past pain from previous miscarriages haunted me, making it hard to fully embrace the present.

On October 30, 2019, during a routine check-up, I requested an ultrasound because I hadn't felt my son move as much. At thirty-eight weeks, having gained a significant amount of weight, I was concerned. The hospital admitted me for monitoring and induction, but after twelve hours, there was no progress. I was faced with the option of a C-section, which I resisted.

After three days of labor, a compassionate nurse explained that my son's heart rate was fluctuating, and I needed to consider a C-section to avoid further risk.

I dreaded the thought of having a C-section and was resisting because this was not in the plan for me. My whole pregnancy was perfect. I wasn't prepared or advised that I would have to have this. So to find this out the day of my delivery was a bit of a surprise for me. Don't get me wrong, I don't knock any woman for having a C-section—as for myself, I just envisioned myself pushing out my child.

However, after the nurse advised me of my son's heart fluctuating, I agreed, and with my partner by my side, I was wheeled into the operating room.

The C-section revealed that my son's cord was wrapped around his neck three times, which explained the decrease in his movements. Holding him on my chest for the first time was pure joy. I knew God had guided us through this journey, and I was overwhelmed with gratitude. On November 1, 2019, my life changed forever. I became a mother.

All I could think was, "I'm a mother now. I'm a mother now." The smell of him was so fresh. I was so attached, holding his hand and letting his small little fingers grip mine. His skin was so soft; his hair was so beautiful and curly. His eyes met my eyes and we were just staring at each other. This felt so surreal—everything I prayed for was right before my eyes. I couldn't believe it.

Looking at my son as my family sat across from me, I was met with so much undeniable joy. November 1, 2019, my life was changed. I was now a mom.

Infertility is a journey marked by both profound heartache and unexpected hope. For many, it is a path fraught with pain and frustration, moments that challenge our strength and resilience. My story, as I share in *Glowing Through What We Go Through*, is a testament to this journey—a narrative of struggle, yet one that reveals how we can rise above our most difficult moments.

The pain of infertility is more than physical; it is deeply emotional and mental. Each miscarriage felt like a personal betrayal, a cruel reminder of dreams deferred. The weight of repeated loss bore down on me, not just as a series of unfortunate events but as a profound trauma that reshaped my sense of self. Each loss brought with it a wave of grief, leaving me to grapple with an array of emotions both overwhelming and disorienting.

Navigating through this pain, I found myself questioning not just my body, but my worth and my future. In moments of solitude, I confronted the harsh reality of my situation, often wondering if I would ever find solace. The emotional toll was immense—grief became a constant companion, and the hope I once had felt elusive and distant.

Yet, within this heartache, I discovered resilience. Each setback, while painful, became a catalyst for growth. The struggles and the bittersweet moments taught me about the strength that lies within vulnerability. Through countless nights of tears and reflection, I began to see that while the path was marred by loss, it was also illuminated by the power of perseverance.

My journey through infertility was not just a battle against physical limitations but a quest for mental and emotional healing. I learned that true strength is not in avoiding pain but in embracing it and finding a way to move forward despite it. The trauma of repeated miscarriages forced me to confront my deepest fears and uncertainties, but it also sparked a transformation. This transformation was not instantaneous; it required patience, self-compassion, and a steadfast belief in my ability to endure and eventually overcome.

In sharing my story, I endeavor to offer a beacon of hope to others facing similar struggles. The journey through infertility is undoubtedly challenging, but it is also an opportunity for profound personal growth. By facing the trauma head-on and allowing ourselves to heal, we can find a deeper sense of purpose and strength. The path is not linear, but it is one that, when navigated with courage and resilience, can lead to a future filled with renewed hope and possibilities.

In the journey of life, we all encounter moments when our dreams, hopes, or aspirations seem to be abruptly and harshly snatched away. For women who have experienced miscarriages, the pain of losing a child can feel like a profound and personal tragedy. Yet, the same principles that apply to navigating such a deep loss can be extended to any woman facing the sudden or unexpected abandonment of her dreams or goals.

It's essential to recognize that what may initially appear as a curse or a catastrophic ordeal can, in fact, be a powerful stepping stone towards transformation and triumph. The key lies in how we choose to navigate these challenges and how we harness our inner strength to move forward.

First, it is crucial to embrace the pain. Acknowledge and honor your feelings of loss, grief, or disappointment. Avoiding or suppressing these emotions only prolongs the healing process. Allow yourself the space to grieve, but also understand that this pain is a natural part of your journey.

Seeking support and guidance can also play a vital role in this process. Just as I found solace in the care of Dr. Jones and the support of my loved ones, seek out those who can offer empathy, encouragement, and practical advice. Surround yourself with people who believe in your potential and are willing to walk alongside you through your healing process.

Redefining your path is another critical step. Use your experience as an opportunity to reassess and redefine your goals. Sometimes, a setback can reveal new directions or passions that were previously hidden. Embrace this as a chance to realign your aspirations with your evolving self.

Finding the silver lining in your struggles can offer profound insights. These experiences often provide valuable lessons about your own resilience, strength, and capacity for growth. Recognize that overcoming adversity can lead to a deeper understanding of yourself and your purpose.

Building resilience is another crucial aspect. Allow your setbacks to fortify your resolve. Each challenge you face and overcome builds your capacity for resilience and adaptability. Use this newfound strength to tackle future obstacles with confidence and determination.

Celebrating small victories along the way is important. Acknowledge and celebrate every step you take towards healing and achieving new goals. Each victory, no matter how minor it may seem, is a testament to your courage and perseverance.

Finally, trust the process. Understand that your journey, though fraught with obstacles, is unfolding as it should. Sometimes, the path to success is not a straight line but a winding road full of unexpected turns. Embrace the journey with faith and patience.

In conclusion, the path from heartache to triumph is not linear, but it is paved with opportunities for growth and self-discovery. By embracing the pain, seeking support, redefining your goals, and celebrating your progress, you transform what initially feels like a setback into a powerful catalyst for personal transformation. Just as I eventually found joy and fulfillment after my trials, you too can emerge victorious, glowing through what you are going through and creating a future that reflects your strength, resilience, and unwavering spirit.

Reflective Pause
Finding Hope in the Storm

Take a moment to reflect on your journey through adversity and the sources of hope that have sustained you. Use these questions to connect with your inner strength and find clarity in your path forward.

✳ What has been your most significant source of hope during challenging times?

_____

_____

_____

_____

✳ How do you process grief, and what strategies help you move forward?

_____

_____

_____

_____

✳ Reflect on a time when you found strength you didn't know you had. What did that experience teach you?

_____

_____

_____

_____

✳ How has adversity shaped your perspective on life and its possibilities?

_____

_____

_____

_____

✳ What does "hope" mean to you, and how can you cultivate it daily in your life?

_____

_____

_____

_____

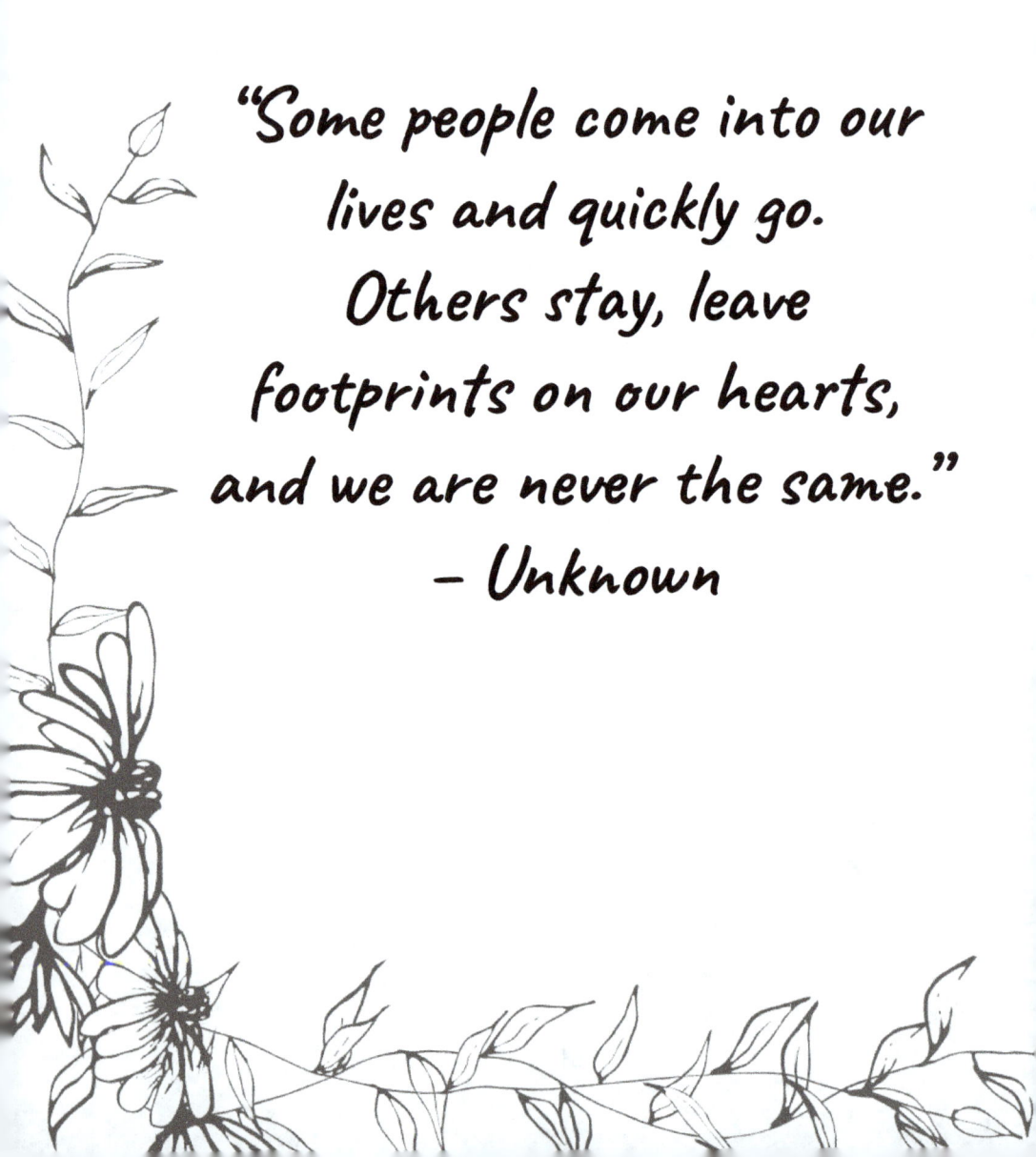

"Some people come into our
lives and quickly go.
Others stay, leave
footprints on our hearts,
and we are never the same."
– Unknown

CHAPTER 4
True Colors Revealed
Navigating Betrayal and Friendship

Betrayal is a unique kind of pain. It's not just the act of someone breaking your trust—it's the ripple effect it creates in your life. It forces you to question everything: your relationships, your judgment, and even yourself.

Whether it's a close friend, a family member, or a partner, betrayal often comes from someone you trusted most, making the sting even sharper. For many, it's not just the loss of a relationship—it's the loss of a belief, the comfort of thinking someone would always be in your corner.

Countless people have shared stories of betrayal—of friends who turned out to be anything but friendly, of confidants who weaponized their secrets, and of relationships that once felt unshakable but crumbled in an instant. What these stories reveal is the complex and often messy process of uncovering true loyalty and learning how to set boundaries.

When the Mask Comes Off

For me, the sting of betrayal came from a friendship I thought would last forever. She wasn't just a friend—she was like family, someone I trusted implicitly and leaned on during my darkest moments. But as time went on, cracks began to form, revealing truths I didn't want to see.

Have you ever had a friend who felt more like a sister or family? That's how close I was to my best friend, who I will call Kate for the sake of peace and who, at one point, meant the world to me. We were inseparable, sharing laughter, secrets, and life's ups and downs. Conversations that stretched for hours filled our time together, as no topic was off limits.

We talked about anything from family matters as young adults, to sibling disagreements, to our intimate dating or love life. Details were always juicy as we left no room for crumbs. Everything we went through was put on the table. Our conversations were true, real, and uncut. We didn't hide or fake the funk about anything, or else the other would know. We talked about everything life presented to us. Our bond was a safe haven and a sisterhood.

Kate was there for me in some of my darkest moments and, likewise, I was there for her in some vulnerable moments. Knowing that I had a sister friend that I could talk to about almost anything was refreshing.

For instance, I remember a time when I confided in her on the phone while discovering some news from my boyfriend at the time, who was up to no good. I was ending my shift at work, which was an overnight shift from ten p.m. to six a.m. I told her I was about to leave and go catch him in his trap of lies he was feeding me. As I told her my plan to leave work and go straight to his house, she interrupted me and said, "Friend, please don't go by yourself, come get me and I'll go with you."

Although I had my mind made up as I rambled through my thoughts of rage at that time, the urgency in her voice as she told me to come get her persuaded me to listen to her request. When I got off work, I did just that and picked her up first so she could ride with me. To my surprise, she was dressed down with sneakers on and her hair tied back in a ponytail. She had on no jewelry, which was not like her normal self. She had Vaseline on her body and face and was ready to go to war and have my back if needed. Before she got into my car, she handed

64

me the Vaseline, as well as a pair of sneakers. I chuckled as I put the Vaseline on my face and then put on the pair of sneakers. I had already changed out of my work uniform prior to leaving my job. Without question, I knew right then and there she had my back. From that day on, I had a newfound respect for our friendship. This overall experience made me feel confident in our sisterhood. I felt a connection and a safe place, where there was a sense of value and trust within our bond.

The fact that she was ready to support my shenanigans and get down to the bottom of things with me went a long way. Needless to say, that very day, I was able to discover some information that was very important for me to know. Through it all, she was there for me while offering sound advice and encouragement that I needed to hear as a friend.

But like many friendships, cracks started to form beneath the surface—cracks that I tried to ignore for the sake of preserving the bond. What I didn't realize at the time was that these cracks would eventually split open, revealing a betrayal I never thought I would see coming. Some of the cracks that I noticed were deeply rooted within her inner being. You know? It was just a natural part of who she was. Kate always enjoyed gossiping about the next person or speaking poorly on a previous relationship. She was the one who eagerly had all the tea and did not mind spilling it. This often made me feel uneasy, because if she could talk about someone she once considered her close friend, I always felt she could easily do the very same to me, although we were very close.

It started with small things. We gossiped often—mostly her, but I played along, even when I knew the things she shared were hurtful or unnecessary. She often revealed intimate details about people we both knew, things that had nothing to do with me, and I found it unsettling. There was a darkness in the way she spoke about others, and even though it made me uncomfortable,

I brushed it off. I convinced myself that the bond we shared was strong enough to overlook these red flags.

I guess I was influenced by the way she always seemed to show up for me whenever I expressed the need for a friend or confidant at the drop of a dime. No matter what it was that I was going through, she always seemed to be there. So taking this into consideration, I allowed many things I normally would not let slide get a pass. I would say I held our friendship on a pedestal and I know she did as well. Her family grew to be my family and vice versa.

But deep down, I knew. If she could speak that way about people she was once close to, what was stopping her from doing the same to me? For instance, we had a mutual friend within our circle, and there were times when she and our mutual friend would go through spells of not speaking to one another. When telling her side of what happened in regards to them not being on speaking terms, I knew there was way more to the story than she was giving. This would be confirmed after hearing from our mutual friend. Then it all eventually made sense.

I felt that her behavior was disturbing and petty. I almost felt like she held back on the truth at times to cover up her own insecurities she was facing. It was kind of like she felt pleased by talking about everyone else's life.

At times, I would even find myself taking a step back just to preserve my personal space and well-being. Sometimes I just needed a moment to myself to gather a collective of observations.

I noticed that whenever I took these steps back, she would still call and check on me even if she felt I would not respond. The less and less I made myself easily available to her, the more curious she would become. It was almost as if there was a need for her to know what was going on with me.

The answer came one day when she called me urgently, interrupting a pivotal moment in my life—a training session for a new job that I had worked hard to secure. She left several frantic voicemails, insisting I call her back. Concerned, I stepped away, expecting to hear something serious. Instead, what I got was a conversation so petty, so absurd, that I was left speechless. "Someone said you have yellow teeth," she blurted out, without any sense of the ridiculousness of the situation. I wasn't offended—I knew it wasn't true. But I was baffled by the pettiness of it all.

Setting aside the gossip itself, Kate's actions left me feeling hurt, betrayed, and almost speechless. I had an overall feeling of annoyance more than anything. The vibe that I was getting from this situation was that Kate wanted to bring me down. I thought to myself. "Do I really want to stoop down to her level or should I rise above this?" At this stage of metamorphosis in my life, I chose to rise above this foolishness. I knew where I needed to go with this, and I followed through.

My words were subtle but my tone was clear. In my confusion, I asked, "Who said this?" But she danced around the question, refusing to name anyone. The more she evaded, the more it dawned on me: there was no "someone." She was the source of the gossip. That revelation hit me hard, but at the same time, it brought clarity. This person, who I had once trusted implicitly, was no friend at all. She had been tearing me down behind my back, just as she had done to others.

I felt there was some envy or hate coming from her end, causing her to act out in this way. Being a friend of Kate for so long, I knew exactly her jealous and spiteful ways. I never cared for that side of her but I knew it was a part of her nature. And although I was saddened by this behavior, I was not surprised by it, which was the final nail in the coffin for my ultimate decision. I knew I had reached the end of our friendship, especially since I could sense in my spirit that she was the source of the conspiracy. I'd had enough of Kate and her evil ways—every fiber in my mind, body, and soul led me to go back to everything I'd witnessed within our friendship up to this very moment. I had sudden flashbacks occur right before my eyes, showing me different, similar scenarios of how she treated others, including me. I was no different from all of our other mutual friends and connections that she stabbed in the back. So this very moment was more so a lesson to me to better choose the people who I allow into my immediate presence. I was no longer going to allow anyone with these negative characteristics to be that close in my circle like that again.

The moment was a turning point for me. I began to pull away, distancing myself emotionally and physically. Slowly but surely, I cut her out of my life, realizing that this friendship was toxic. During this period, she experienced a personal loss, and while I once would have rushed to console her, I found that I no longer had the energy or desire to do so. It was a clear sign that I had moved on. I was finally free from the weight of our unhealthy connection.

During this process, I did not feel guilty at all. I felt it was necessary towards my growth and towards my letting go of something that no longer served my presence. I felt this was the beginning of a new life and a new me. The new me was no longer allowing myself to settle for unjust or toxic relationships. In asserting this, I felt a sense of relief. I invited peace, love, and harmony into my life, as I'd realized the true importance of protecting all three. So in order to live in peace, love, and happiness, I had to first let go of anything that was the complete opposite of that. This was a true learning process. However, it was very necessary, because I learned that not everyone deserves the right to be within your space and it's perfectly okay to acknowledge that.

As difficult as it was to let go, it was also empowering. I realized that clinging to a friendship that no longer served me was holding me back. The betrayal wasn't just about her actions—it was about my own failure to listen to my intuition. I had seen the signs but chose to ignore them because I didn't want to face the truth. The truth that this person I had let into the deepest parts of my life was not who I thought she was.

What was overlooked was the extreme gossiping and ultimate betrayal of close mutual friends. The fact that she always had a story about someone's life and found a way to focus on their downfalls or dark moments. It's like she shined the light brightly on others' vulnerable and darkest moments, yet what was interesting was the fact that she withered away from her own vulnerable moments, while often pretending she was perfect or better than the next. This was a huge red flag which displayed major insecurity.

The betrayal wasn't a single moment of rupture; it was a slow unraveling, like a thread quietly pulled until the entire fabric of our friendship came undone. When the truth finally came to light, it hit me like a tidal wave. I had been deceived, and the betrayal felt personal. It wasn't just an assault on our friendship—it was an assault on my ability to trust, on the very foundation of who I believed her to be.

Even though I didn't want to admit it, there were times where I saw this pain carry over towards certain areas of my life. Physically, I was still the same person. Spiritually, my connection with God and my growing church family was continually deepening and improving. But I was still emotional wounded and at times, I would find myself comparing other close friendships to my previous friendship with Kate, knowing that I was betrayed by her. I just had my guard up with everyone. This was a battle within myself that I eventually overcame. I began to draw myself more into a closer relationship with God by going to church more and listening to the Word. I also became part of a loving, welcoming prayer group within my church and family. I overcame my emotional wounds because of God and because my true family and friends till this very day have continued to show up and show out, while making positive contributions towards my relationship with them.

There were many other moments when I took a deep look back on our overall relationship. Kate had a way of drawing you into the drama even if you didn't want to be involved. As she continued to vent to me about previous relationships, topics, or situations, I always knew there was hurt and spite on her end but as a friend, I allowed her to vent. Eventually, after multiple similar scenarios or events continually happening with different people she was once close with, it began to weigh on my heart that maybe Kate was the source of the problem.

What I noticed with these friends was that they were going places. Some graduated multiple times, gaining more educational degrees; some were growing happy families; some were celebrating career success. In each case, the main thing that stuck out was the envy she showed of others' success. It was almost like she didn't want her friends to grow and be successful. She was always there for you when you had a down moment in your life—the best of friends during your downfall. But when you were growing, maturing, and getting more and more successful, that's when I'd notice the hate within her.

That's when the gossiping came, when the negative and evil ways of her started to unveil. It never seemed to fail. I realized that she was a very clingy and jealous person once she saw you were growing up and away from her. She could not stand it. She secretly envied all of her close friends and hated the fact that they eventually outgrew her ways.

Have you ever had a friend who is always there for you during your darkest moments but never around to celebrate your highs in life? Please take the time to look closely at your friends.

For a long time, I wallowed in the pain. I replayed every conversation in my head, wondering how I could have missed the signs. I questioned my judgment and wondered if I was foolish for trusting so deeply. The bitterness festered inside of me, and in the process, I built walls around myself. I withdrew, preferring the safety of isolation over the risk of opening myself up to others. But isolation, while comforting in its predictability, soon became a prison. I realized that I wasn't just punishing her—I was punishing myself.

I didn't necessarily retreat from the world and relationships around me. In fact, I grew closer to a childhood friend that has always been in my corner throughout all phases in my life. Till this day, we are still standing strong. This experience allowed me to focus more on the people who are always there for me while learning to only pour into others that are able to pour back into me.

Don't get me wrong, this process was not easy because it opened my eyes more to my surroundings in a way that I never observed before.

I realized that I had to weed out whatever God allowed me to weed out of my life. Whatever he continued to show me about myself and others who I felt were close to me. There came a pivotal moment of transformation for who I was becoming. And within this transformation, some people had to be let go so I could grow. Even other long-term friendships outside of Kate were chosen to let go due to personal growth within myself. This experience allowed me to dive deeper into who I am as a person. Do I want to be surrounded by positivity or negativity? Do I want to surround myself with friendships or people who are stuck or stagnant, or do I want to continuously grow and prosper? These are the questions I would ask myself during the process of eliminating stagnation in my life. Some people had to be let go, which is a process of growth.

It was then that I recognized I had to make a choice. I could either let the betrayal define me, or I could rise above it. I knew the latter wouldn't be easy, but I also knew that the pain I was experiencing wasn't something to just endure—it was something to learn from. Rising from betrayal is not a straight path. There were days when the sting of her actions still burned, days when I felt the anger bubble up inside me, threatening to drown me in its intensity. But slowly, I began to rebuild.

The message that I decided to receive for my well-being was to keep smiling, keep shining, and to move on. This betrayal was the beginning of my self journey. I had to use this situation as a testimony that sometimes, it's important to let go of any hindrance and sabotage that was once somehow connected to you. Whether it may be from a friend, an associate, a colleague, or a family member. The key is learning not to let that betrayal hold you hostage any longer in your suffering or in beating yourself up. Yes, instead, turning around your outcome is essential for your success.

When I started thinking with this mindset, not only did it allow me to take my power back, but it also allowed me to no longer feel victimized. Once I no longer felt like a victim, I was able to unlock the doors of diving deeper into who Tejumade is. This led me to gain a closer connection to my relationship with God, which was a vital process necessary for me to grow and heal.

Through this, I was able to be thankful for a lesson learned, which slowly helped me become a better person towards myself. It was time for me to start listening to my inner self and stop ignoring signs. You know, sometimes we can immediately see these red flags and situations where we know better, but for safety or sometimes even comfort, we can tend to adapt or accept it blindly, even when we see the messages right before our very eyes. That right there is a big no no moving forward. It's vital to accept and acknowledge everything we see right before our very eyes with no shield whatsoever.

When you shield your eyes and try to blind yourself to messages that appear right before you, this only invites pain and dishonor to your life. In order to have a credible, fulfilling life filled with character respect and virtue, these are things you must take into perspective. If you don't make necessary things such as respect and honor a priority in your life, then you leave room for unnecessary events to take place that could have been prevented.

So the lesson is to guard your life and space accordingly, because no one else can do these things for you. Set your standards high and treat others the way you would like to be treated. When it comes to friendships and relationships, stop expecting the best outcome to come from the not-so-best person. Practice self-love to attract what you would like to embody as a reflection of you.

All this is an important part of self-reflection. I took the necessary time to look at myself in the mirror profoundly and deeply. Doing this became my daily routine and as I continued doing so, I enjoyed being here.

Rebuilding wasn't just about forgiving her—it was about forgiving myself. I had to let go of the belief that I was to blame for what happened. Her betrayal was a reflection of her, not me. This realization allowed me to shift from a place of anger to a place of growth. I started to see the experience not as an end, but as a beginning—a painful but necessary catalyst for my personal evolution.

As shared previously, the hardest part of healing was learning to trust again, not just in others, but in myself. I had doubted my instincts, questioned my judgment, and wondered if I was capable of discerning who was truly worthy of my trust. But slowly, I began to reconnect with my intuition. I reminded myself that one betrayal did not mean I was broken.

What I didn't expect was the spiritual transformation that would follow. The deep wounds of betrayal forced me to look inward, but also upward. In the midst of my pain, I found solace in my faith. I realized that while human relationships may falter, my relationship with God was unshakable. The betrayal had stripped away many illusions, but in that barren emotional landscape, I found a deeper connection with my Creator. My faith became my anchor in those dark times, and through prayer and reflection, I began to heal.

Looking back, I see the betrayal not as a devastating loss, but as divine redirection. God allowed that friendship to crumble because it no longer served my growth. The betrayal, as painful as it was, had been necessary for me to rise into a new season of my life. It taught me that sometimes, in order to bloom, you must prune away the dead leaves and rotten stems that no longer support your growth.

Through this experience, I've learned several lessons, and I share them in the hope that they may help others:

1. **Betrayal is about them, not you.** It's easy to internalize betrayal as a reflection of your worth, but it's not. The actions of others stem from their own insecurities, fears, and struggles. You can't control their behavior, but you can control how you respond to it.

2. **Trust can be rebuilt.** Betrayal shatters trust, but trust is not irreparably broken. It takes time, and it requires patience, but you can learn to trust again—both in others and in yourself.

3. **Forgiveness is freedom.** Holding onto anger and resentment keeps you trapped in the past. Forgiveness doesn't excuse what was done, but it frees you from the chains of bitterness.

4. **Adversity reveals strength.** Betrayal can feel like it will break you, but it also reveals a strength within you that you may not have known existed.

I now walk with a deeper understanding of myself and others. The betrayal that once seemed to define me has become a chapter in my story, not the whole book. I'm still learning and growing, but I no longer see betrayal as the end. Instead, it's a beginning—a painful, necessary part of the journey towards a stronger, more resilient self.

To anyone who has experienced the sting of betrayal, know this: you are not alone. The pain you feel is real, but it will not last forever. You have the power to rise above it, to learn from it, and to emerge stronger on the other side.

Reflective Pause
Unveiling Truths and
Rebuilding Trust

As you think about the themes of betrayal and resilience, consider the lessons these experiences have taught you. These questions are an opportunity to explore the importance of boundaries, forgiveness, and self-worth.

✳ Think about a time you experienced betrayal. How did it affect your sense of trust and self-worth?

_____

_____

_____

✳ What red flags or warning signs did you overlook in a relationship, and why?

_____

_____

_____

✳ How have you set boundaries to protect your peace and emotional well-being?

_____

_____

_____

✳ In what ways can forgiveness serve as a pathway to freedom for you?

_____

_____

_____

✳ What lessons have you learned about the types of people you want to surround yourself with?

_____

_____

_____

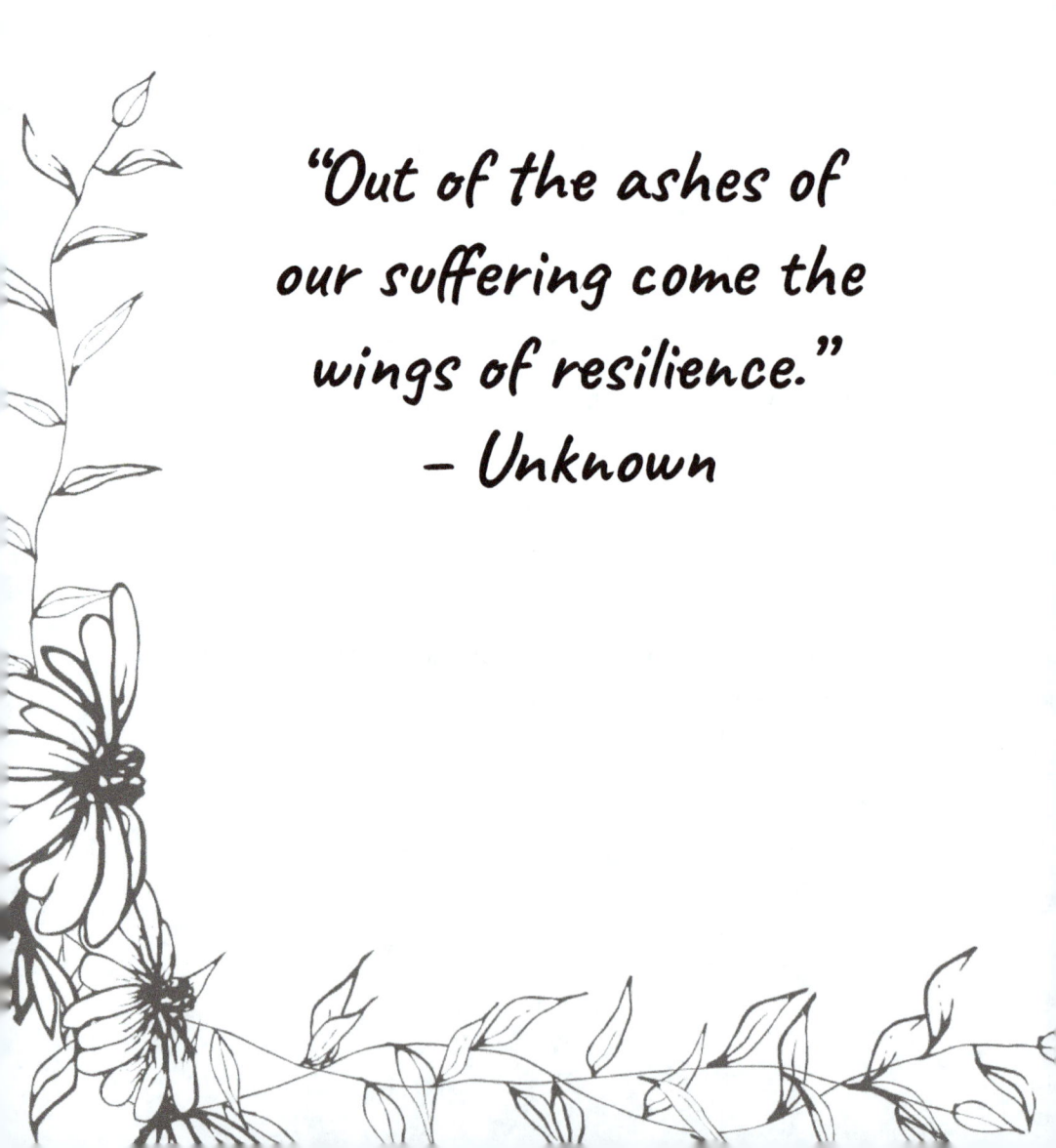

"Out of the ashes of our suffering come the wings of resilience."
– Unknown

CHAPTER 5
Rising from the Ashes
Overcoming Career Setbacks

The Crushing Weight of Setbacks

Career setbacks can feel like the ultimate defeat, especially when you've poured your heart and soul into a dream. Whether it's a missed opportunity, a failed project, or a dream job slipping through your fingers, the emotional toll can be overwhelming. It's a punch to the gut, forcing you to reevaluate your worth and the path you thought was set before you.

One of the most notable stories of resilience in the face of career setbacks is that of **Steve Jobs**. In 1985, after leading **Apple Inc.** to incredible success, Jobs was ousted from the very company he had founded. The decision was a devastating blow to Jobs' career and his identity as a tech visionary. To be removed from a company he helped build must have felt like losing a part of himself.

But instead of accepting defeat, Jobs found a way to rise from the ashes. He went on to start **NeXT**, a company that would ultimately bring him back to Apple years later. Jobs' journey was a testament to the power of reinvention and perseverance, showing that even the greatest setbacks can be opportunities for growth and innovation.

Jobs later returned to Apple in 1997, when the company was on the brink of bankruptcy, and transformed it into one of the most valuable companies in the world. His story is proof that a setback doesn't have to be the end—it can be the beginning of something greater.

My Own Setback Story

For me, a career setback wasn't about being ousted from a company, but about having a dream I had worked so hard for seem to unravel before my eyes. My first book, a deeply personal project I had invested years of my life into, was taken down from major platforms due to a series of miscommunications. I had felt like I was standing on the edge of a cliff, watching my work slip away, and there was nothing I could do to stop it.

The weight of that moment was heavy. I had invested not only money, time, and energy, but my heart and soul into this project. The setback shook me, making me question if my dream was even worth pursuing. But as I sat in the quiet aftermath, I realized something that I hadn't seen before: this setback wasn't the end—it was the beginning of a new chapter.

Like Steve Jobs, I realized that I had the power to rise above this challenge. I could either stay down, defeated by the loss, or I could use the experience as a stepping stone to build something even better. It wasn't an easy decision, but it was the right one.

The Dream Deferred

Writing has always been my passion—a means of self-expression, a creative outlet, and the path to fulfilling a dream I've cherished for as long as I can remember. When I finally reached the milestone of publishing my first children's book, it felt surreal, like I was living my dream. Holding that book in my hands and seeing it available on some of the biggest platforms felt like the culmination of everything I had worked for. The joy was beyond words, and sharing this accomplishment with friends, family, and followers filled me with pride.

I was excited, especially knowing that my book carried an important message. It was a children's book about diversity and inclusion—topics that hold great meaning, particularly in a world that often feels divided. Witnessing my work being recognized on a major platform with a growing distribution gave me a sense of fulfillment I'd only ever dreamed of.

The reason this meant a lot to me was because I'm a child of an immigrant, as my father is originally from Nigeria. Although I was born in the United States, there were many times as a young child where I had stood out from the crowd. Picture yourself as a child with a unique first and last name that only a few could pronounce. People often stumbled across the pronunciation of my name, some even mimicked or made fun of it. Imagine the hurt, pain, anger, or discomfort this could cause a child who was simply born into a beautiful, unique family. **Tejumade**, which my father always told me means *"fix your gaze on the crown."*

I found myself always taking the necessary time to correct and enlighten others. At times, this effort took a toll on me, but I knew it was necessary to clear up others' ignorance. However, as an adult, I truly know and recognize the beauty of my name and I cherish that my father took the time to name all of his daughters with much substance. So for this very reason, this book being on the shelves truly meant the world to me.

Knowing that I was able to share my story with many others in this world who are just like me, unique in their own way, yet still loved by God, was a major accomplishment that was near and dear to my heart.

The Devastating News

I'll never forget the moment my publisher informed me that a significant issue had come up—a problem that would change the course of my journey as an author. However, she kept me in the dark, stating she wasn't sure why this happened, and passed the blame over to the publishing platform. Because I lacked insight about the intricacies of publishing, I took her word for it and faded away in my sorrow and disappointment. What I know now was that she had registered my ISBN on one publishing platform under my first and last name and she also registered my ISBN on another platform under her company's name, which she hadn't any right to do as I hired her as a "work for hire" and also because she should have known that her action was a direct violation of the rules and would lead to termination if discovered, as it was recognized as copyright infringement.

So, just when I thought I was prospering, everything slowly came to a halt. It was almost like I was being pushed to a standstill, waiting for the next steps which never came.

Due to these complications and poor account management, my book was pulled from major platforms. This devastating news came with additional consequences. My account with one of the most influential book-selling platforms was not only closed but permanently banned. That moment felt like the ground was ripped out from under me. I had achieved a lifelong goal, only to watch it slip away overnight.

I couldn't fathom the thought that the masterpiece I created was being taken down. "How could this possibly be happening to an amazingly written book with an uplifting message?" I asked myself in shock as I recalled my actions to ensure that my dream had a chance to flourish and grow. I invested not only in myself but in my dream when I hired someone who was supposed to be a professional, someone knowledgeable about the process and steps to publishing.

Feeling Powerless and Alone

Days turned into weeks as I tried to wrap my mind around what had happened. The publisher, who had assured me they were handling everything, had actually opened my account in their company's name while also using their email address for all correspondence. Because of this, I had no insight into what went wrong or why my book was removed. The publisher remained silent, unresponsive to my questions while I stayed up night after night, poring over every page of my manuscript, every piece of correspondence. I felt abandoned, and worse, my dreams of having a career on these significant platforms felt crushed. I was left alone with only vague apologies and the unsettling reality that my dream was slipping away.

In moments like these, I felt as though all my hard work— the countless hours I spent writing, editing, and perfecting my book—had been for nothing. Thousands of dollars had been invested in this dream, and now it felt as though I was holding the pieces of something that was shattered beyond repair.

Despite the heartache, I kept pushing myself to see the silver lining. My book was still available on some other platforms, albeit not as widely. I tried to find comfort in that, but it felt like a small consolation compared to what I'd lost. I couldn't shake the feeling of betrayal, nor could I forget how much I had trusted this publisher, only to find out later that I'd been taken advantage of.

A Prayer for Guidance and the Strength to Move Forward

In the midst of my despair, I turned to prayer. I needed guidance, clarity, and a sense of peace to help me decide what to do next. I prayed for the strength to rebuild my dream and for a way to find healing and hope. I also felt the need to write another book that shared my story of resilience, strength, and overcoming, yet I was scared to invest in myself and another person representing themselves as a publisher or self-publishing coach. Although this was my thought process at that very moment, I knew I had to move past this fear because my tribe was waiting for my book to be released in hopes of learning from my story.

Then, something shifted. I felt a spark—a small but determined fire inside me reignited. This was not the end of my journey; it was simply an obstacle I had to overcome. I didn't know how or where to start, but I knew I couldn't let this setback define me. There had to be another way forward, and I was willing to search for it.

Meeting Reea: A Beacon of Hope and Knowledge

It was around this time that I connected with Reea, an experienced publisher who had a reputation for helping authors reach their full potential. Our first meeting felt different from anything I'd experienced with my previous publisher. Reea welcomed me with open arms and an open mind. She listened, not only to my story but to my vision, my goals, and my fears. Her understanding and kindness were refreshing.

Reea offered to educate me on the publishing process, something my first publisher had never done. I was hesitant at first—still wary from my previous experience—but Reea's genuine approach put me at ease. She wasn't just interested in publishing my book; she wanted to empower me as an author.

From our first meeting, Reea shared insights that immediately made a difference. I quickly learned the importance of managing my own accounts and maintaining control over my work. She explained that as an author, I should always have ownership of my account and direct access to my source files. This was something I hadn't realized before, and it opened my eyes to just how much I'd been missing.

Learning and Growing with Reea's Team

With each session, Reea and her team guided me through the complexities of publishing, marketing, and the business side of being an author. They explained what it meant to truly build a career as a writer—not just publish a book, but create something sustainable and impactful.

For the first time, I was given tools and strategies to position my book for success. Reea helped me develop a clear understanding of my target audience, refine my message, and identify the value my book could bring to readers. I was learning not only how to write a book but how to write a book with impact. Let me say that again. I was learning not only how to write a book but how to write a book with impact.

Reea's commitment went beyond the basics. She taught me about monetizing my work and creating additional revenue streams, a concept that was entirely new to me. She explained how an author could leverage their book to open doors for speaking engagements, workshops, and even online courses. Her knowledge transformed my view of what it meant to be an author.

A Newfound Confidence

With Reea's guidance, I finally began to feel confident in my ability to succeed as an author. Each day felt like a step towards reclaiming the dream I had almost lost. The tools and strategies I learned from Reea felt like pieces of a puzzle that I had been trying to assemble blindly. Now, I had a clear picture of what my journey could look like, and the courage to pursue it wholeheartedly.

Reea even introduced me to the concept of bestseller strategies and ways to increase book visibility. This information was invaluable, and as she taught me, I felt a renewed sense of purpose. I finally felt equipped to build a successful career as an author, one rooted in my own goals and driven by my dedication and newfound expertise.

Reflecting on My Past Mistakes and Moving Forward

As I looked back on my first experience with publishing, I realized that I had put too much faith in someone who did not have my best interests at heart. It was painful to accept, but acknowledging this truth was liberating. For the first time, I stopped blaming myself for what had happened. I had been naïve, yes, but that didn't mean I deserved what had happened to me.

This reflection allowed me to see the experience as a lesson. It taught me the importance of taking ownership of my work, of understanding the process, and of choosing partners who value transparency and integrity. Moving forward, I would no longer settle for anything less.

A New Beginning

Armed with everything I'd learned, I was ready to embark on a new chapter of my career. I chose to work with Reea, not only because of her expertise but because of her genuine desire to help authors succeed. With her guidance, I felt empowered, supported, and capable of achieving my goals.

Looking back, I realize now that the setback I endured was necessary. It was a test of my resilience, a storm that had to pass so that I could see the sunshine that followed. The experience has strengthened me in ways I never anticipated, and it has prepared me for the success that lies ahead.

I no longer see the loss of my first account as the end of my dream. Instead, it is a lesson in resilience, a reminder that sometimes we have to face setbacks to discover our true strength. Now, I am moving forward with faith, with courage, and with the unshakeable belief that I am capable of rising above any challenge.

Perhaps you've felt this way, too. Maybe you've been in a place where the path forward felt blocked, where a betrayal or unexpected setback left you questioning everything. You may have poured your heart and soul into something, only to see it threatened, or even destroyed, by forces beyond your control. It's as if you're standing in the eye of the storm, watching pieces of your dream scatter. And in that moment, it's easy to feel lost or tempted to walk away.

But here's what I want you to hold onto: every storm eventually passes. No matter how fierce, no matter how turbulent, storms make way for clarity and calm. And it's in that clarity, after the storm, that we often find the true purpose behind our trials. When life tests us, it's asking us to grow, to step into a version of ourselves that can withstand the next level of our journey.

Your dreams are worth fighting for. The setback you're facing today, the challenge that feels insurmountable, is simply one chapter in a larger story. Imagine if every great figure—every dreamer and pioneer—had stopped at their first defeat. Imagine if they had let one disappointment define them. There would be no stories of triumph, no breakthroughs, no evidence of the power of resilience. Even if you feel you've hit a wall, take a step back and look at the bigger picture. Setbacks don't mark the end of your journey; they're merely signposts, guiding you to new strengths and perspectives, carrying lessons and a chance to refine your vision. Sometimes our greatest breakthroughs come from moments that seem like breaking points.

When I was at my lowest, when it felt like my dreams had been shattered, I found a new path forward by learning from what had gone wrong. I rebuilt from that place, not just because I had to, but because my dream mattered too much to give up. And so does yours.

So, if you're in the middle of your own storm right now, if things feel out of control or far from what you envisioned, trust that you are being prepared for something greater. Keep moving forward. Hold onto your purpose. Gather strength from what you're going through. You are stronger than you think, and every challenge is simply building you for what's next.

Let this chapter of your life be the one where you rise above, where you learn, adapt, and keep pushing forward. The path may be winding, but it's leading you towards the person you were always meant to become. Keep going. The rainbow after the storm is waiting for you, and it will be even more beautiful than you ever imagined.

Prayers most certainly get answered—sometimes not in the order or way we want them to, but they still get answered. Something told me to reach out to my lawyer for an update concerning the legal letter he drafted and sent out on my behalf, concerning my first book being removed. So I did just that, hoping for good news. However, after speaking with him, I was advised that he heard no response from the other party as of yet.

Although this was not the news that I was waiting to hear, hope still lived within me. After our follow-up call had ended, I provided the updated info to my writing coach Reea. Not necessarily the news I wanted to deliver to her as an update but it was necessary for her to know. We both concluded our conversation with hopeful insight and beliefs that eventually everything will work out. Although my goal was to remain positive and hopeful, the human in me was growing tired.

Fast forward to the following week, which was the early part of November of 2024. Reea and I had just concluded a scheduled meeting regarding the next steps of my new book with her. What was concluded with this meeting were key things that needed to be done in order to move forward regarding the current status of my account. One of the main things we discussed was how imperative it was for me to get full access to both of my accounts that were created by my previous publisher. So during that week, I was adamant to make sure I did just that. Although this was a challenge for me, I proceeded with much diligence and care, knowing how important it was to get this matter resolved, by reaching out to my previous publisher who I hadn't spoken to in a while and mentioning all of the things I needed from her.

During this interaction with my previous publisher, I felt encouraged, not only because everything went well with receiving what was rightfully mine but also because I was taking charge of the outcome for my current situation.

After receiving full access to all of my accounts that were created by the previous publisher, I immediately changed all of my passwords and alerts so that all notifications would go to me and me only. It was this same day that I decided to take the necessary time to review all of my missed emails, and to my pleasant surprise, there was a reactivation email from the largest platform advising me that they had decided to overturn their previous decision concerning my account with them.

All I could do at this moment was jump for joy. I was literally stunned to read such news. But I knew that all of my praise and honor went to God because without him, none of this would be possible. So I just started to say thank you to God repeatedly. I felt so relieved to hear such great news!

To think that I would not have even known of this amazing news if I never took charge to gain all of my access to my accounts . . .

There would have just been notifications sitting there, waiting for me to receive them. I was beyond grateful for God's divine intervention in this pivotal moment of my life. It was at this very moment that I knew that meeting Reea was a blessing from God. Sometimes he places the right people in our lives at the right moment for a reason and there is no denying the fact that everything is working out according to his will.

You see, I needed the information that I was lacking and a little push and nudge in the right direction, and Reea was definitely that nudge behind me that I needed. She helped me apply pressure where needed, and I am more than grateful for her guidance during this process.

When I think of all the accomplishments I've managed within the course of five months of working with Reea, it inspires me to never give up even when you feel you've reached a snag in the road. In this short time, I was able to turn around many things that got in the way of my dream.

A moment of reflection reveals to me that sometimes storms come in the process of our growing season. Within the process of this season, that storm can be used as a test that will eventually turn into a testimony.

In sharing my story with you, I want you to understand that no matter what may come your way, in the midst of that season, you will eventually shine and persevere through it all. Sometimes in the moment, it may not always feel that way. However, coming from a person who made it through many storms, I can attest that those moments don't last forever.

I've shared with you some of the most intimate moments of my life that I chose to place in this book as a testimony to help others that may have experienced a setback. Just remember, it's not over, it's not the end of the world, and most importantly, you will get through it and your strength will outweigh the odds. You are your biggest cheerleader and you are also your biggest critic.

So in saying this, please remember to root for yourself no matter what, even in the midst of a storm. Eventually, that sun is going to come out and illuminate your whole world with its brightness. You got this!

Reflective Pause
Rising Strong After Setbacks

Challenges and setbacks can teach us resilience and perseverance. Reflect on how your own journey has been shaped by obstacles and how you can use them as stepping stones towards your dreams.

* Describe a time when a career or personal setback felt overwhelming. How did you navigate through it?

_____

_____

_____

_____

* What internal resources (like faith, resilience, or creativity) helped you rebuild after a loss?

_____

_____

_____

_____

* How do you define success, and has that definition evolved through adversity?

_____

_____

_____

_____

* What steps can you take today to reclaim control over a dream that feels lost or deferred?

_____

_____

_____

_____

❋ Reflect on a moment when a failure or disappointment revealed an unexpected opportunity. What did you learn?

_____

_____

_____

_____

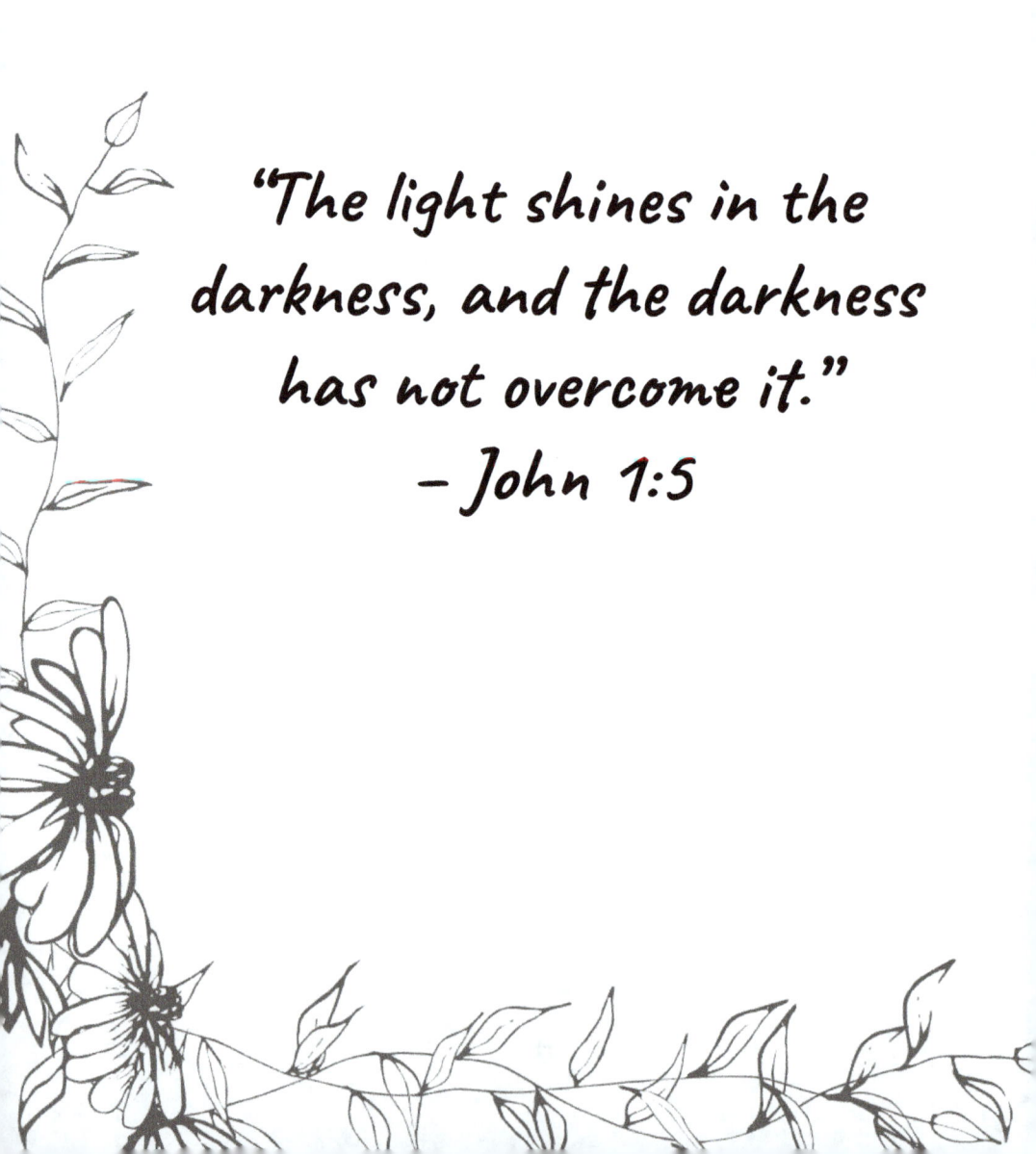

"The light shines in the
darkness, and the darkness
has not overcome it."
– John 1:5

CHAPTER 6
Finding Light in the Darkness
Spiritual Transformation

The Chains That Bind Us

Addiction is a powerful force that can take many forms—substances, behaviors, or even thought patterns that control our lives and prevent us from stepping into the fullness of who we are meant to be. For many, addiction is not something that is obvious to others, but an internal struggle that quietly shapes their decisions and steals their peace.

Whether it's an addiction to substances, habits, or even unhealthy relationships, it's easy to feel bound by forces that seem impossible to overcome. But the good news is that through prayer, community, and the strength we find in God, it is possible to break free. The power of transformation through faith is a testament to how we can overcome even the deepest struggles.

One powerful example of overcoming addiction comes from **Tyler Perry**, the well-known actor, producer, and writer. Before his success, Perry struggled with many challenges, including a deep battle with **addiction to negative thought patterns** and **self-destructive behaviors**. Perry often talks about how he spent many years struggling with anger, resentment, and fear, which led him to a dark place emotionally and spiritually.

Tyler Perry's turning point came when he found the strength to surrender his pain to God and seek out community. He credits his faith and the support of a church community as key elements in breaking free from his destructive behaviors. Through prayer, therapy, and the love and support of others, Perry was able to heal and go on to create one of the most successful media empires in the world. His journey is a reminder that, no matter how bound we feel, there is always hope and freedom available through the power of faith and community.

Finding Light in the Darkness: My Journey

In moments of uncertainty, many of us turn to something—or someone—to fill the void. For me, it was psychics. For others, it might be a toxic relationship, overindulgence, or compulsive behaviors. My journey began as a search for clarity during a confusing time but quickly spiraled into an unhealthy dependency that consumed my finances, emotions, and spiritual life.

For years, I was trapped in a cycle of dependency on psychic readings. It started innocuously enough—I was going through a transitional period in my personal life, unsure of which romantic relationship to pursue. My boyfriend and I had reached a standstill as he was grappling with a major loss. Despite offering him my unwavering love and compassion, his pain left him unable to receive it, no matter how hard I tried. Recognizing his need for space and time to heal, I had to step back and honor that process.

During this challenging period, I turned to my best friend, who had always been a comforting and attentive listener. However, our dynamic began to shift. My best friend found himself wanting more than just the "best friend" role in my life and I realized so did I, as we were both struggling to reconcile our feelings and hold onto the title we'd carried for so long.

One day, I saw an ad for California Psychics and thought, why not give it a try? That first call was eye-opening—the psychic seemed to know intimate details about me and my situation that I had never shared. Intrigued, I found myself calling back again and again, seeking answers, predictions, and guidance.

What began as a casual exploration quickly spiraled into an all-consuming obsession. I started calling the psychics daily, sometimes multiple times a day, racking up hundreds of dollars in charges each month. I became addicted to the thrill of hearing predictions that would come true, validating the psychics' abilities in my mind. No matter how much I spent, I always felt the need for one more call, one more insight into my future.

This dependency took a heavy toll. Financially, I was draining my resources, putting myself in precarious situations just to afford the next psychic session. But the true damage was spiritual. By regularly seeking counsel from these self-proclaimed seers, I was opening myself up to dark, ungodly forces, as the Bible warns against. Eventually, I began experiencing spiritual warfare, a battle I was unequipped to fight on my own.

It was only when I hit rock bottom, facing severe financial and emotional strain from my psychic habit, that I finally recognized the need for change. But the path to freedom would require not only a profound spiritual transformation but mental and emotional as well, which would challenge me to the core of my being.

Addiction comes in many forms—shopping, social media, alcohol, or even relationships. At its core, it's often about escaping discomfort or seeking answers where there seem to be none. My addiction to psychics may seem unusual, but the root cause was the same: I was looking outside of myself, and outside of God, for what I thought I lacked.

Turning to Prayer for Guidance

In my darkest hour, I turned to prayer, which led me to my pastor, for guidance. Imagine yourself looking at your bank account with fifty dollars in it and having the urge to deplete that fifty dollars for the sake of needing or wanting to hear a prediction with a premier psychic. When I found myself at this pivotal moment, I knew something was wrong. This was my turning point and I promised myself to put an end to this. This is when I reached out to my pastor in confidence, ashamed of my behavior but with the willingness to make a change.

Finding Hope Through Spiritual Guidance

My pastor's response was filled with compassion and wisdom. He listened without judgment, explaining that my reliance on psychics had opened doors to spiritual forces that were not of God. This resonated deeply with me—I had felt the weight of spiritual warfare but didn't know how to name it.

He encouraged me to take a series of intentional steps:

* **Renounce the Past**: I must publicly renounce my involvement with psychics, declaring my intention to sever ties with those influences.

* **Repent and Reconnect**: Through prayer and repentance, I must ask God to forgive me for seeking guidance outside of Him.

* **Commit to Change**: I must commit to deepening my relationship with God through baptism, joining my church community, and immersing myself in His Word.

I knew I needed spiritual guidance to overcome this struggle in my life and my pastor listened patiently as I poured out my story, my desperation palpable. He understood the gravity of my situation and the spiritual implications of my actions.

Offering compassion and wisdom, he explained that by repeatedly seeking counsel from psychics, I had unwittingly opened doors to the ungodly realm—forces that were now wreaking havoc in my life. This spiritual warfare was a direct consequence of my choices. Essentially, it's a fight between the forces of good and evil in the unseen spiritual realm, where believers use their faith and reliance on good to resist the negative influence. It was creating mayhem in my life due to necessary boundaries being broken. However, I was assured that there was a way out.

Breaking free required me to pray and take the tangible steps outlined by my pastor. The path to freedom would require a complete surrender to God and a commitment to spiritual disciplines. Knowing this, I took the prideful step towards deliverance by getting baptized and joining my church. After doing so, I learned to repent while asking God to forgive me for all of my sins. I gave my life fully to Christ and began to see myself changing slowly.

Additionally I renounced my involvement with the psychics, closed those open doors, and actively fought against the enemy's influence through prayer and the Word of God. Guided by my determination to change the trajectory of my life, I unsubscribed from psychic mailing lists, deleted their numbers from my phone, and reached out to trusted friends to hold me accountable. These actions, paired with my growing faith, helped me reclaim control over my life. The more I took action in regaining my power, the more I was able to see a growing change in my life. My ability to resist calling the psychics grew as I replaced that urge with the Word of God and prayer. I was shocked when weeks of not calling led to months, and when months turned into years that was a huge accomplishment. I knew I was changed when I was offered a 100-dollar credit by email from one of the psychic networks advising that they missed me. I kindly declined the offer for the sake of my well-being and new beginning.

Learning to Pray with Power and Authority

Under the guidance of my pastor, I began to learn how to pray with power and authority. He taught me to declare God's truth over my life, standing firm in His Word. It was through this journey that I learned how to confront the spiritual forces that had kept me bound in addiction, whether it was to psychics or any other form of escape. I learned to reject the forces that fed my dependency and started claiming the freedom God had always promised me.

At first, the battle felt overwhelming. I didn't just struggle with addiction—I struggled with the spiritual weight of it. The thought that I could break free seemed impossible, especially when the pull to escape my pain was so strong. Maybe you've felt that too—like something outside of you is controlling your decisions, pulling you into a cycle of behavior that doesn't feel like your own. It's easy to feel defeated, believing there's no way out. But as I continued on this journey, I realized something profound: with God's help, change is always possible.

One powerful message from my pastor really shifted my perspective. He said, "When the Spirit of the Lord speaks to us, we must listen and act, even in the midst of fear and uncertainty." This resonated with me deeply because addiction often keeps us paralyzed by fear. It feeds us lies—telling us that we need something outside of ourselves to feel whole. But courage doesn't mean being fearless. True courage is being willing to act, even when fear is present, and choosing to do what's right even when we feel unsure.

In 2 Timothy 1:7, we are reminded, "God has not given us a spirit of fear, but of power and of love and of a sound mind." When we allow ourselves to truly grasp this truth, it becomes clear: we are equipped to face any battle. For me, this was a turning point. I began to realize that, with the Holy Spirit's guidance, I could walk confidently in the authority God has given me, no matter how heavy the addiction seemed.

Maybe you can relate to the weight of addiction that feels too heavy to bear. It might be fear, shame, or even the belief that you are not strong enough to overcome it. But I am here to tell you, you don't have to be strong enough on your own. God has already equipped you. You don't have to fight this battle in your own power. When you lean into Him, you will find the courage to take the next step.

I had to stop letting fear dictate my choices. I learned that if I remained stuck in fear, I would never move past the addiction that had its grip on me. But when I chose to take steps forward in faith, trusting that God's plan was greater than my circumstances, nothing could stand in my way.

And maybe, like me, you've felt the weight of your struggles lifting as you begin to walk in your purpose. As I continued to pray, I started to feel a shift. The spiritual oppression that had been weighing me down began to lift. The grip of addiction slowly loosened, and I found a newfound freedom in my heart and mind. It wasn't an instant fix, but each prayer and each moment of surrender moved me closer to the woman I was meant to be.

If you're struggling with addiction—whether it's to substances, habits, or the search for external validation—remember that God's truth can break the chains. The freedom you long for is already within your reach. It starts with taking that first step, even if it's small, and trusting that He is with you every step of the way.

Rediscovering the Power of God's Word

Alongside the intensive prayer, my pastor emphasized the importance of immersing myself in the Word of God. He encouraged me to read the Scriptures daily, to meditate on the promises and truths found within its pages. As I did so, I began to see the world through a different lens, one that was grounded in the eternal, unshakable foundation of God's truth.

The more I studied the Bible, the more I realized the grave error of my ways. Seeking guidance from psychics was a direct violation of God's command to avoid such. I had been deceived, opening myself up to spiritual forces that were never meant to have a hold on my life.

This story I shared is my testament to the transformative power of surrendering to the divine and trusting in the guidance of the Almighty. I learned that when I found myself entangled in the allure of worldly advice and the "thrill of the moment," I had the courage to take a step back and reflect deeply on my priorities. This moment of self-reflection was a pivotal turning point, which allowed me to recognize the true source of wisdom and peace through my committed relationship with God.

It takes immense strength and resilience to let go of unhealthy attachments while seeking the counsel of the divine. The ability to demonstrate this fortitude, making the conscious decision to distance myself from the ungodly influences that had previously captivated me, allowed me to surrender. Although it was not easy, it was a necessary step towards reclaiming my spiritual footing while aligning my life with the principles of faith.

As I leaned into my relationship with God, I discovered the profound comfort and clarity that comes from trusting in the Lord's plan for my life. The Scriptures became my ultimate guiding light, illuminating the path forward and providing the wisdom I so desperately sought. This immersion in the word of God was transformative, for it allowed me to discern the difference between godly wisdom and worldly advice, empowering me to make decisions that were in harmony with this test of faith.

The support of a committed church family played a crucial role in this journey of transformation. Learning to lean on my pastor's guidance and the surrounding community of believers offered the spiritual nourishment and encouragement I needed to navigate through these challenging times. Their unwavering presence and the shared experience of walking the path of faith together served as a powerful reminder that I was never alone in my struggles.

Let this story be a testament to the resilience of the human spirit and the boundless potential for growth and positive change that lies within each of us. No matter how deep the valley or how daunting the climb, with the steadfast support of the divine and the community of believers, we can overcome any challenge and emerge stronger, wiser, and more deeply connected to the source of all wisdom and love.

In life, as we continue our journey, we must learn to remain steadfast in our faith. My connection to the Lord remains unshakable, which has allowed my commitment to the Word of God to become unwavering.

It is important to lean on the strength of your church family, draw inspiration from the Scriptures, and trust in the plan that the Almighty has for our lives. For in doing so, you will only continue to transform your tests into powerful testimonies, inspiring others to embark on their own journeys of spiritual growth and renewal.

As I move forward, I have learned to constantly remind myself that I am a child of the Most High, a warrior of faith, and a beacon of hope in a world that so desperately needs the light of my resilience and the power of my testimony.

Throughout my journey, I will continue pressing forward, while keeping my eyes fixed on the divine, knowing that the Lord walks beside me every step and filling my heart with the courage to face any challenge that may arise.

I hope in sharing this story that you too can find solitude in sharing your own stories, which can be a true gift to the world, a testament to the transformative power of faith, and a reminder that with God, all things are possible.

Reflective Pause
Discovering Light in the Darkness

The darkest moments often hold the seeds of transformation. Take time to explore your connection to faith, purpose, and inner peace as you answer these reflective questions.

✳ When have you felt most spiritually lost, and how did you begin to find your way back?

_____

_____

_____

✳ What practices help you stay connected to your sense of purpose and inner light?

_____

_____

_____

✳ How has your faith, or lack thereof, influenced how you face life's challenges?

_____

_____

_____

✳ What does "light in the darkness" mean to you, and how have you experienced it?

_____

_____

_____

✳ If you could offer one piece of wisdom to someone currently in their own dark moment, what would it be?

_____

_____

_____

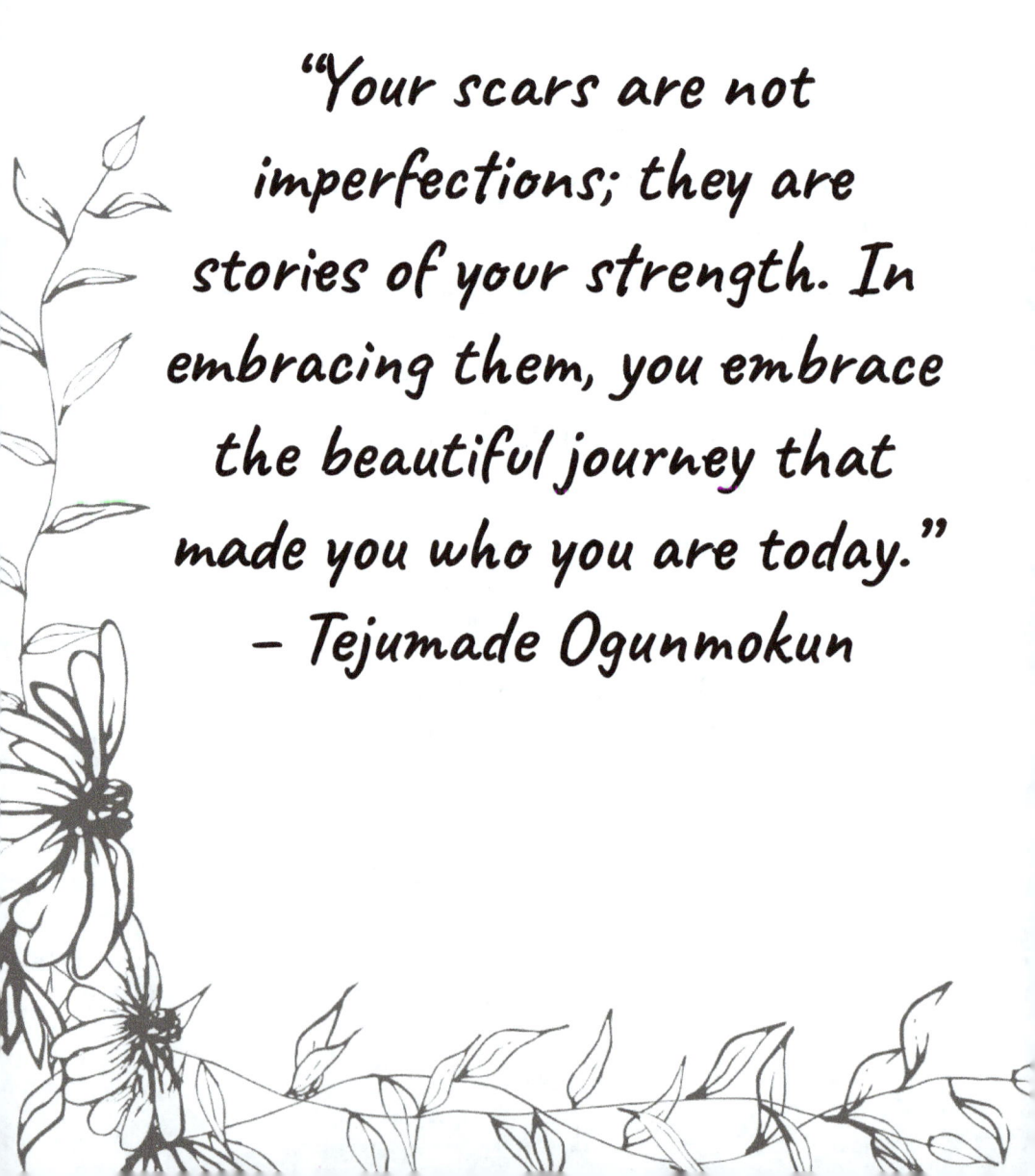

"Your scars are not imperfections; they are stories of your strength. In embracing them, you embrace the beautiful journey that made you who you are today."
— Tejumade Ogunmokun

Chapter 7
Imperfectly Perfect
Beneath the Surface, Flaws and All

I remember the first time I caught a glimpse of my scar in the mirror after my C-section. No offense to anyone, but I felt obese. In fact, I thought I was huge. My thighs were larger than I had ever imagined, and when I looked down, all I could see was my stomach. Being a former model with a figure I had always taken pride in, this reflection felt almost unrecognizable. I took a step back from the mirror, stunned by the sight before me. Was this really me? Everyone assured me I would get back to my "normal self" eventually, but at that moment, I wasn't sure. I was consumed by disbelief and trapped in a reality that didn't feel like mine.

The scar on my body felt like more than just a physical mark. It was a symbol of the monumental shift in my life. As I traced its outline with my fingers, emotions bubbled to the surface—grief, insecurity, awe. I had brought a beautiful new life into the world, but in the process, it felt as though I had lost a part of myself. The woman staring back at me was unfamiliar. Where had the confident, independent, unstoppable version of me gone?

The days that followed were anything but easy. Recovery was a slow and humbling process. The doctors insisted I rest and take care of my healing body, but that meant relying on my partner for almost everything—lifting our baby, completing household chores, even making a simple cup of tea. While I was immensely grateful for his unwavering support, I couldn't shake the feelings of guilt and frustration. I hated feeling so dependent. I was used to being the one in control, always moving forward, always accomplishing. Now, I felt like a shadow of myself, unsure if I would ever return to the vibrant woman I once was.

One evening, I decided I'd had enough of sitting idly by. Against my better judgment, I attempted to pick up our newborn son from his crib. The pain that followed was so sharp it nearly brought me to my knees. My partner rushed to my side, gently taking our baby and placing him in my lap. He sat me down and reminded me of the doctor's advice: I needed time. I needed to heal. But all I could feel was helplessness and frustration. Was this what my life would look like now—a constant reminder of what I couldn't do?

That evening, as my partner rocked our baby to sleep, I finally broke down. I shared everything with him—my insecurities about the scar, my struggle with dependency, my fear of losing myself. He listened patiently, holding me close and reassuring me that I was doing my best. His words were a balm to my weary soul, but I knew the real work had to come from within. I had to find a way to reconnect with myself, to rebuild the confidence and strength that felt so far away.

Rediscovering Myself Post-Pregnancy

The journey back to feeling like myself wasn't linear. It was messy and emotional, but it was also transformative. I started by seeking guidance from a close friend who happened to be a nutritionist. Together, we crafted a diet plan—not one focused on rapid weight loss, but one centered on nourishing my body. Each meal became an act of self-love. I wasn't just feeding myself; I was honoring the body that had carried and delivered my child. Slowly, I began to see food not as an enemy but as a source of strength and renewal.

When the doctor finally gave me the green light to exercise, I approached it with caution and care. My first steps were literal— gentle walks around the neighborhood. The fresh air on my face, the ground steady beneath my feet, these small moments felt monumental. Gradually, I worked up to more movement, celebrating every bead of sweat as a sign of progress. It wasn't about chasing a number on the scale; it was about reclaiming my strength, step by step, rep by rep.

Shifting My Perspective

What surprised me most about this journey was how much of it was mental. The physical healing was challenging, but the emotional work required a different kind of strength. For a long time, I viewed my scar as a flaw, a blemish on the version of myself I once admired. But as I moved through my healing process, my perspective began to shift. This scar wasn't a flaw— it was a testament to my resilience, a badge of honor that told the story of what my body had endured and accomplished. Slowly but surely, I started to see its beauty.

Motherhood itself became my greatest teacher. In the quiet moments, holding my baby close, I discovered a love so profound it made all my insecurities seem insignificant. His laughter became my light on the darkest days, a reminder that joy often resides in the simplest moments. I began to see my body not as something to critique, but as something to celebrate. It had brought life into this world. It had persevered through pain and transformation. It was, and always would be, enough.

A New Definition of Beauty

I realized that beauty isn't about perfection. It's about authenticity. It's about the courage to embrace every part of who we are, even the parts we once struggled to love. This understanding didn't come overnight. It took time and intentionality. But as I stood in front of the mirror one day, preparing for our first family photo,

I felt a shift. My hair was done, my nails polished, and for the first time in a long time, I felt radiant. Not because I looked perfect, but because I saw myself—truly saw myself—as strong, resilient, and beautiful.

That photo captured more than just a moment; it captured a transformation. It was a visual reminder of my journey from insecurity to self-acceptance, from dependency to independence, and from healing to thriving. It reminded me that while motherhood had changed me, it hadn't diminished me. If anything, it had expanded my capacity for love—for my child, for my partner, and most importantly, for myself.

Lessons in Transformation

Through this journey, I've learned some invaluable lessons. I've learned that it's okay to lean on others for support. Healing, whether physical or emotional, isn't something we're meant to do alone. I've learned the importance of self-compassion, of giving myself grace in moments of doubt and struggle. And I've learned that strength isn't about doing it all; it's about knowing when to rest and when to rise.

Motherhood taught me to embrace imperfection. It showed me that the messy, chaotic moments are often where the deepest beauty lies. It taught me to find joy in the small things—in the giggles of my child, in the quiet moments of connection with my partner, in the simple act of showing up each day with love and intention.

The Beauty of Imperfection

Now, when I look in the mirror, I see more than just a scar. I see a story. I see strength. I see a woman who has weathered storms and come out stronger on the other side. I see a mother, a partner, a creator of life. And most importantly, I see someone who is imperfectly perfect.

To anyone reading this, I want you to know that you are enough. Your scars, your stretch marks, your tired eyes—they are all part of your unique story. They don't diminish your beauty; they enhance it. They tell the world that you've lived, loved, and grown. And that is something to celebrate.

As I close this chapter, my heart is full of gratitude. Motherhood has changed me in ways I never expected, but it has also taught me the value of embracing every part of myself. In the eyes of my son, I found not just my reflection but the truest, most beautiful version of me. And I hope that in your own journey, you too will find the beauty that has always been within you.

Reflective Pause
Celebrating Transformation

Transformation, whether through motherhood or other life changes, often challenges us to embrace new versions of ourselves. Take a moment to reflect on your own journey— what you've overcome, what you've gained, and how you've grown. Use these questions to deepen your understanding of your unique story.

✻ How have life's transitions—big or small—shaped your perception of yourself?

_____

_____

_____

✻ What "badges of honor" in your life tell a story of resilience and strength?

_____

_____

_____

✻ In moments of change, how do you practice self-compassion and patience with yourself?

_____

_____

_____

✻ How can you reframe perceived imperfections as symbols of growth and love?

_____

_____

_____

✻ What small, meaningful moments in your life remind you of the beauty in your journey?

_____

_____

_____

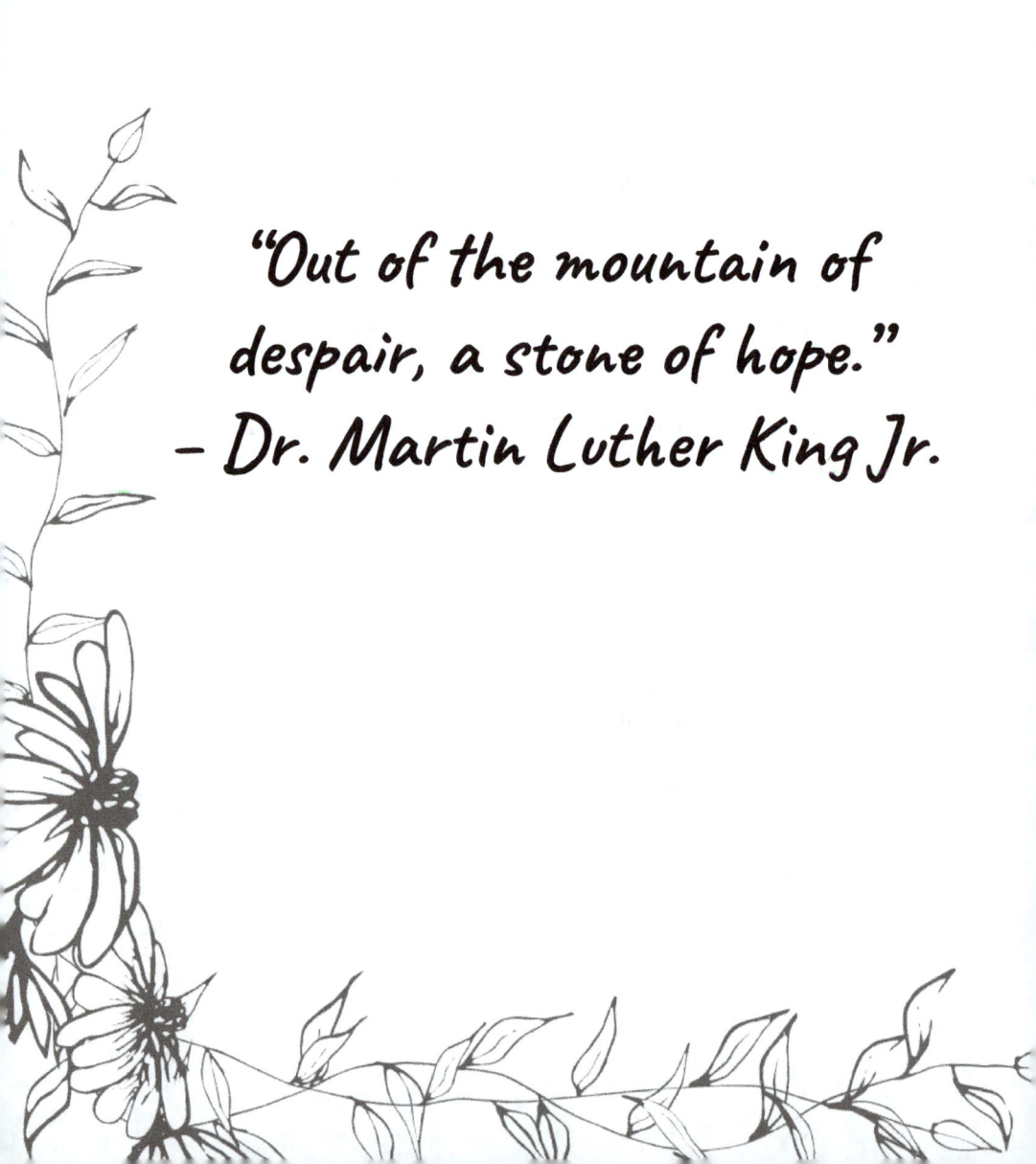

"Out of the mountain of despair, a stone of hope."
— Dr. Martin Luther King Jr.

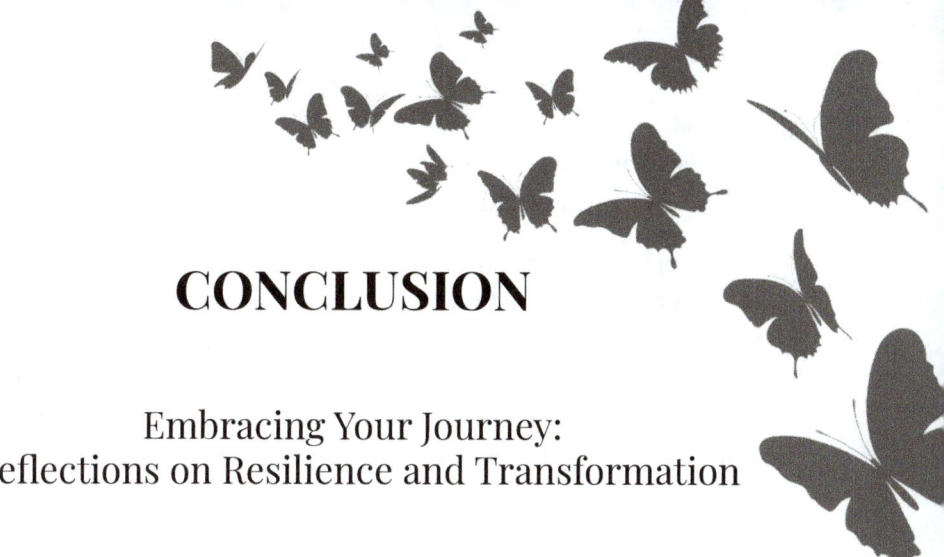

CONCLUSION

Embracing Your Journey:
Reflections on Resilience and Transformation

As I bring this story to a close, I invite you to reflect on the journey we've shared. It hasn't been an easy road, but every challenge, every setback, has been a testament to the strength that lies within each of us when we choose to persevere. My story is not just my own; it is proof of the power of resilience, faith, and the beauty that can emerge when any one of us chooses to lean into growth instead of defeat.

Throughout this book, you've walked with me through heartbreak, betrayal, setbacks, and moments of spiritual confusion. We've seen how the divine presence of God, prayer, and sheer determination can lead us through the darkest of valleys and back into the light of purpose and fulfillment. It's a reminder that the storms of life don't have to break us; they can, instead, make us stronger, more compassionate, and more connected to our true purpose.

One of my favorite teachings comes from Sarah Jakes Roberts, who once said:

"Your past is not your prison; it is the platform God will use to showcase His grace and glory in your life."

These words remind us that no matter what we've been through, our struggles can become the foundation for something greater. They are not meant to define or limit us but to prepare us for the calling God has placed on our lives.

If there is one truth I hope you take away, it is that you are never alone in your battles. God's grace has carried me when I was weak, and His plan has always been greater than my pain. For every struggle I faced, there was an opportunity to transform and grow—a chance to surrender my fears and step forward in faith. I want you to know that this same opportunity exists for you, even in the moments when hope seems distant.

So, as you close this book, I challenge you to consider what it means for your own life. Reflect on the obstacles you've overcome and the person you've become as a result. Embrace the belief that the best version of you is continuously being refined. Choose to rise up, pray fervently, and connect with those around you who uplift and inspire. Remember that every trial has a purpose, and every triumph is a testament to the unwavering power of faith.

May you walk forward with courage, knowing that you are supported by a divine strength that never falters. Let your story be a beacon of hope, a reflection of grace, and a reminder that you, too, are capable of glowing through whatever you go through.

ACKNOWLEDGEMENT

Philippians 4:6
"Do not be anxious about anything, but in every situation, by prayer and petition, with thanksgiving, present your request to God."

This scripture resonates deeply with every step I take each day. First and foremost, I want to give all my honor, praise, and thankfulness to God. I owe everything to You. It is through Your divine intervention and guidance that I have been able to turn many situations in my life around. You saved me, directed my path, and guided my footsteps. For that, all the glory must go to You!

You called me to write, and though I didn't know what I was meant to write at the time, You led me every step of the way. You guided me to create my very first children's book, *Fearfully & Wonderfully Made*, published in 2023—a celebration of diversity. Shortly after, You inspired my second book, *Beneath the Surface*, published in 2024. And now, here I am, writing my third book, *Glowing Through What We Go Through*, which I hold so dear to my heart. I never imagined the plans you had in store for me. Your vision and purpose for my life far surpass anything I could have envisioned for myself.

You have a remarkable way of showing up and showing out, and for that, I am endlessly grateful. You've empowered me to pick up my pen—not only to heal myself but also to bring healing and inspiration to others. This journey has been nothing short of amazing, and I owe it all to You.

To my mother, Mary, and my sisters, Moji and Sade: thank you for being my inspiration. Your guidance, support, and perseverance have deeply impacted me, even when you didn't realize I was watching. Thank you for never giving up and for being living examples of strength and resilience.

To my father, Taiwo: thank you for being such a strong influence in my life. You raised us to be the beautiful Black queens we are today. I am forever grateful for the cultural pride you instilled in us, including our meaningful Nigerian names. Those names remind me of who I am and where I come from. Your love and wisdom are gifts I will always cherish.

A heartfelt thank you goes to my publishing team. It truly takes a village to bring a book to life. To Dara Publishing LLC, your commitment to excellence in editing, formatting, and all the finishing touches has been invaluable. None of this would have been possible without your dedication and hard work.

To my publisher, book coach, and now friend, Reea Rodney: words cannot fully express my gratitude. Your belief in me and this project has been life-changing. You've been more than just a phenomenal publisher; you've been a guiding light, pushing me beyond limits I didn't know I could surpass. Your unwavering support, constructive feedback, and incredible attention to detail have transformed my vision into reality. I've learned so much from you, and I know that our connection was divinely orchestrated. Thank you for being such an integral part of my journey.

I cannot forget to mention my amazing church family, Speaking Spirit Ministries, led by Pastor Fred and Ingram Wyatt. Through your transparency in teaching and impactful ministry, I was able to fully submit myself to God, which led to a major shift in many areas of my life. Thank you, from the bottom of my heart, for all you continue to do within your ministry and community. Your dedication and service are deeply appreciated.

To my amazing boyfriend and biggest supporter, Ishon: thank you for always cheering me on. Your comfort and encouragement, especially during those late nights of writing, mean more to me than words can express. I love you endlessly.

And to my son, Imari, my heart and my greatest inspiration: Mommy loves you so much. You are the reason I push myself every day. Knowing that I am your mother fills me with strength and purpose. Everything I do is for you, and I hope to make you proud.

ABOUT THE AUTHOR

Tejumade Ogunmokun is a multifaceted woman of God, deeply devoted to her roles as a mother, sister, daughter, aunt, soulmate, teacher, model, and friend. Her greatest joy is being the mother of her amazing son, Imari, who brings light and purpose to her life.

With an associate's degree in business administration and currently pursuing her bachelor's degree in psychology, Tejumade is committed to personal and professional growth. She is the proud owner of *Touched by Tejumade Beauty & Cosmetics,* where she uses her God-given talents in hairstyling, makeup artistry, and fashion expertise to empower and uplift women in her community.

Tejumade's love for writing and literature has always been a cornerstone of her life. Through her transformation journey, she discovered the healing power of journaling and has since used her pen to inspire, uplift, and bring hope to others. Writing with purpose, she aims to help others heal by sharing her own experiences and triumphs, turning life's challenges into powerful testimonies.

An unstoppable and phenomenal woman of faith, Tejumade is on a continuous journey of learning, growth, and self-improvement. Her mission is to inspire others to rise above adversity and find their inner strength, just as she has.

Dear Reader,

Thank you from the bottom of my heart for purchasing and reading my book. Your support means the world to me and has been a driving force behind my writing journey. I hope this book has touched your heart and inspired you as much as writing it has inspired me.

If you enjoyed the book, I kindly ask that you take a moment to leave a genuine review on Amazon. Your feedback not only helps me grow as an author but also assists other readers in discovering my work.

Thank you once again for your support and for being a part of this journey with me.

Warmest regards,

Tejumade Ogunmokun

www.ingramcontent.com/pod-product-compliance
Lightning Source LLC
Chambersburg PA
CBHW061657120626
46550CB00003B/977